TRANSCENDING TEXTUALITY

PENN STATE
ROMANCE STUDIES

EDITORS
Robert Blue *(Spanish)*
Kathryn M. Grossman *(French)*
Thomas A. Hale *(French/Comparative Literature)*
Djelal Kadir *(Comparative Literature)*
Norris J. Lacy *(French)*
John M. Lipski *(Spanish)*
Sherry L. Roush *(Italian)*
Allan Stoekl *(French/Comparative Literature)*

ADVISORY BOARD
Theodore J. Cachey Jr. *(University of Notre Dame)*
Priscilla Ferguson *(Columbia University)*
Hazel Gold *(Emory University)*
Cathy L. Jrade *(Vanderbilt University)*
William Kennedy *(Cornell University)*
Gwen Kirkpatrick *(Georgetown University)*
Rosemary Lloyd *(Indiana University)*
Gerald Prince *(University of Pennsylvania)*
Joseph T. Snow *(Michigan State University)*
Ronald W. Tobin *(University of California at Santa Barbara)*
Noël Valis *(Yale University)*

TRANSCENDING TEXTUALITY

*Quevedo and Political Authority
in the Age of Print*

ARIADNA GARCÍA-BRYCE

THE PENNSYLVANIA STATE UNIVERSITY PRESS
UNIVERSITY PARK, PENNSYLVANIA

LIBRARY OF CONGRESS
CATALOGING-IN-PUBLICATION DATA

García-Bryce, Ariadna, 1968–
Transcending textuality : Quevedo and political authority in the age of print / Ariadna García-Bryce.
    p.   cm. — (Penn State romance studies)
Includes bibliographical references and index.
Summary: "Examines the political writings of the seventeenth-century Spanish poet Francisco de Quevedo within the context of the social and material practices of spectacle culture"—Provided by publisher.
    ISBN 978-0-271-03775-2 (cloth : alk. paper)
    ISBN 978-0-271-03776-9 (pbk. : alk. paper)
1. Quevedo, Francisco de, 1580–1645—Criticism and interpretation.
2. Quevedo, Francisco de, 1580–1645—Political and social views.
3. Politics and literature—Spain.
I. Title.

PQ6424.Z5G424 2011
868'.309—dc22
2010046246

Copyright © 2011
The Pennsylvania State University
All rights reserved
Printed in the United States of America
Published by The Pennsylvania State University Press,
University Park, PA 16802–1003

It is the policy of The Pennsylvania State University Press to use acid-free paper. Publications on uncoated stock satisfy the minimum requirements of American National Standard for Information Sciences—Permanence of Paper for Printed Library Material, ANSI Z39.48–1992.

This book can be viewed at:
http://publications.libraries.psu.edu/
eresources/978-0-271-03775-2

Para Diego, Luciana y Emilia: lo son todo.

CONTENTS

List of Illustrations   ix

Acknowledgments   xi

Introduction   1

1
Crafting Royal Omnipotence   15

2
The Power of the Passion   47

3
The Agonistic Word   73

4
Vacuous Print   100

Epilogue   137
Notes   141
Works Cited   145
Index   157

ILLUSTRATIONS

1	Andrés Mendo, emblem, "Sic Regat Rex Solvm, vt Sol Regit Polvm," 1653.	16
2	Emblem, "Lvdibria Mortis," 1640.	17
3	Titian, *King Philip II Offering His Son Prince Ferdinand, to God After the Victory of Lepanto*, 1573–75.	18
4	Diego de Velázquez, *Portrait of Philip IV as a Young Man*, 1628.	19
5	Diego de Velázquez, *King Philip IV of Spain*, 1655–60.	20
6	El Greco, *The Dream of Philip II*, 1579.	55
7	Jeronimus Wierix, *Christ Gives the Symbols of Power to Philip II*, 1667.	56
8	Caravaggio, *Doubting Thomas*, 1601–2.	62
9	Juan Martínez Montañés, *Jesús de la Pasión*, 1610–15.	65
10	*Eucharistic Chariot*, 1655.	68
11	Emblem, "Vni Reddatvr, 1640.	115
12	Emblem, "His Polis," 1640.	117
13	Emblem, "Impeditvs Est Sol, et Vna Dies Facta Est, qvasi Dvo," 1666.	120
14	Juan de Noort, *Philip IV Flanked by Religion and Faith*, 1641.	121
15	Emblem, "Ex Fvmo in Lvcem," 1640.	131

ACKNOWLEDGMENTS

MY DEEP GRATITUDE to Alban Forcione for reading the manuscript and offering his wisdom. Heartfelt thanks go to several friends and colleagues for their precious input at earlier stages of the book project: Elisa Sabourian, Rodolfo Aiello, Ramón Mujica Pinilla, Marc Schneiberg, Maureen Harkin, Margaret Greer, Ronald Surtz, and Crystal Chemris. A special word for Carolina Erdocia for undertaking the herculean task of locating well-preserved early modern emblem sources. In addition, I would like to acknowledge the Reed College Dean's Office for its generous financial support and Katie Pelletier for her invaluable proofreading work. I am most grateful, as well, to Penn State's anonymous reviewers for their lucid suggestions. To my parents, Alexandra and José, and to my brother, Iñigo, for standing by me unconditionally, a capitalized THANK YOU. Finally, words cannot express my indebtedness to my husband, Diego Alonso, for his intellectual inspiration and emotional companionship. It is to him and to our daughters, Luciana and Emilia, that I dedicate these pages.

INTRODUCTION

THE INTERCONNECTEDNESS OF WRITTEN WORD, oral address, pictorial representation, theatrical performance, and ceremonial act has received considerable attention from scholars of the early modern period, who have approached the subject from a number of disciplinary perspectives, perhaps most notably those of material bibliography (Chartier, Bouza), response theory (Freedberg; Stoichita), and festival culture studies (Mulryne and Goldring; López). In dialogue with these approaches and their underlying objective of relating cultural production to social practice, *Transcending Textuality* examines the post-Tridentine political imagination through the eyes of one of its principal exponents: Francisco de Quevedo y Villegas (1580–1645). Embedded in the languages of court ceremony, monarchical and spiritual imagery, and religious and classical oratory, Quevedo's political prose imagines politics, arts, and letters as mutually reflecting forms of public exhibition, primordially directed at moving the audience. In the mythical representations of rulership depicted in his royal advice books, as in his satire of Habsburg Spain, which lays bare the fictitious nature of power, Quevedo provides a most productive framework for examining the material and ontological foundations of the culture of display as well as the manner in which it responds to historical change.

From Jorge Luis Borges's renowned affirmations about Quevedo's "grandeza [. . .] verbal" (Borges, *Otras inquisiciones* 61) to recent studies of the ideological and social significance of his *conceptismo* (Gutiérrez; Clamurro, *Language*; Peraita, *Quevedo*), the rhetorical Quevedo has been given fairly consistent consideration. Yet how his verbal craft relates to a larger multidiscursive sphere has, until now, received only scant attention. Linking his political treatises to the visual and plastic arts, to religious and court ritual, and to sacred and secular oratory allows us to unpack an important dimension of his authorial agenda, namely, the attempt to retain in writing the qualities of live performance. Quevedo's work shows a pronounced proclivity for the spectacular: it participates in an organic cultural vision that treats written expression as an extension of oral performance and material display; at the same time, his extreme resistance to incipient modernization denotes preoccupations about the decline of spectacle.

Quevedo writes at what we might call a transitional moment, an epoch in which the familial or personalized distribution of power within the domestic sphere of the king's household begins to be complicated by the emergence of an alternative social model arising with the bureaucratic state, which promotes the impersonal allocation of tasks, "based [. . .] on the dissociation of the position and its occupant, the function and the functionary, the public interest and private interests" (Bourdieu, "From the King's House" 43). Among the significant changes accompanying this trend are the growing protagonism of print and hand-written documents, the increasingly remote or diffuse presence of the king in an expanding state machine, the domestication of the nobility, the rise of the civil servant, the expansion of mediated government, and the appearance of a large-scale public. In contrast with those of his contemporaries who do not see these phenomena as necessarily impeding the effective propagation of authority, Quevedo understands them as signs of social and cultural eclipse.

His bias toward forms of communication predicated upon unmediated control of audience experience and a seamless fusion of cultural and natural bodies is, in fact, consistent both with his belief in feudal models of charismatic leadership and power distribution and with his discomfort vis-à-vis the nascent order based on professional merit, paper communication, the commodification of social capital, and the acceptance of the fabricated nature of culture. Even in the middle years of his career, when he writes the first part of *Política de Dios,* a text that grants at least some of the pragmatic necessities of rulership, the particular ways in which he transforms worldly acts into mythical events set Quevedo apart from other mirror-of-princes writers. Later in his life, he will altogether reject the practice of prudence in favor of an ethos of ostentatious idealism, as good politics comes to be embodied in scenes of martyrdom, pathos-ridden speech, and brazen public action. There is here an evident correspondence between an intensified communicative *energeia* and a politically uncompromising posture. Diverging from other notable figures of the *antiguo régimen,* such as Diego de Saavedra Fajardo and Baltasar Gracián, who negotiate between modern practices and traditional heroic ideals, and who propose forms of prudent conduct that perpetuate established models of authority while adapting to the times, Quevedo harnesses heroism to an aggressive sensoriality that undermines the rationalizing (Weber) and civilizing (Elias) impetus of the emergent state.

If his writing proves a particularly interesting window from which to understand the politics of culture and the culture of politics in Baroque Spain, it is in great measure because, as one of the most belligerent authors of a conflicted time, Quevedo highlights the historical and ideological pressures affecting the performance-centered antiguo régimen. At the same time, the contrast between his exacerbation of these pressures and his contemporaries' somewhat more fluid attitude toward change sheds light on the varied ways in which Habsburg Spain contends with early modernity.

I cannot mention Quevedo's conflict with his era without acknowledging my indebtedness to now classic studies. Lía Schwartz Lerner's foregrounding of the social critical concerns informing his verbal "agudeza" (22), Raimundo Lida's thoughts on his "'modernidad' [. . .] fúnebre" (13), Manuel Durán's commentaries on his subversion of classical poetics (73), and George Mariscal's reading of the epochal tensions lying at the heart of his authorial project (90) have long provided a solid contextualization of Quevedo's cultural program.[1]

Now it is time we made use of the growing body of scholarship on the theatrical qualities of Baroque arts and letters and on the cultural effects of print to further refine our understanding of the profoundly self-conscious manner in which Quevedo's texts think about the deployment of political symbolism in the age of print. The works on which my analysis focuses, Quevedo's major treatises on government, *Política de Dios: Govierno de Christo* (1621–39) and *Marco Bruto* (1631–44), and his foremost political satire, *La Hora de todos y la Fortuna con seso* (1633–35), center upon the act of communication as physical performance. The myriad representations of this act contained in the treatises—for example, the masterful Christian ruler instilling fear in his subjects, the messianic king arousing compassion, the embattled republican orator spurring his audience to rebellion—bespeak an uncompromising defense of the "order of the body" (Berger 147), which our author opposes rather strictly to a lapsed world where the live rapport between speaker and audience is no longer the sole means of political and social influence. That Quevedo's rhetorical ideals involve an alarmist view of emergent modes of circulation is quite blatantly manifest in *La Hora de todos*, which overtly links the decline of "the order of the body" to the expanded use of writing and print.

In sum, Quevedo's work operates at two different levels. At one level, it endorses "a mythical-traditional system" in which "an absolute identity exists between the act of transmission and the thing transmitted, in the sense that there is no other ethical, religious, or aesthetic value outside the act itself of transmission" (Agamben, *The Man* 107). And at another, it points repeatedly and in different ways to the untenability of this ideal in the current political and cultural landscape.

In seventeenth-century Spain, the value of vivid exemplification was widely touted. In direct opposition to a Cartesian grounding of truth in independent thought and the negation of "example and custom,"[2] Counter-Reformation culture, in great measure, anchored truth in palpable illustration and public enactment. It is telling, for instance, that mention is so commonly made of the "colores" of arguments, a reference to their descriptive qualities, which are celebrated as a form of conceptual nuance, painterly amplification being equated with signifying density. Also symptomatic in this respect is the wide-ranging meaning of the word "teatro," both in the ecclesiastical and the secular spheres—Pedro Portocarrero y Guzmán's *Teatro monárquico de España* and Gil González Dávila's *Teatro eclesiástico* being relevant examples. The pervasive *theatrum mundi* allegory can be used to refer to any event, collection of events, or discourse about them.

Tying this emphasis on spectacle to a neofeudal ideology that deliberately set about curbing the secularizing forces of modernization, Antonio Maravall famously understood it as a centralized control mechanism of the Habsburg state. Benefiting from the hindsight of many years of debate about this approach, scholars have had a chance to weigh the merits of dissenting allegations that Maravall's argument yields a deceptively monolithic view of culture as purely apparatus driven (La Flor), against revisionist claims that deem productive its attempt to articulate a relationship between subject and state (Lewis and Sánchez; Spadaccini and Martín-Estudillo). Drawing from both sides of the debate, I attend to the ways Baroque mentalities respond to a common concern about the material and cultural effects of modernization. Where I would distance myself from Maravall's idea of a "guided culture" insofar as this means a top-down process buffered from resistance or critical engagement, I approach Baroque works as being permeated by an instrumental or programmatic self-consciousness (Greer, "Constituting").

Cultural and intellectual endeavors are, indeed, strongly informed by the Ciceronian formula "ut probet, ut delectet, ut flectat" (to prove, to delight, to move) (23) and Augustine's related principle that knowledge and moral worth are not useful unless accompanied by the power to convey (*On Christian* 119). Therein lies one of the central theoretical bases for the pervasively championed idea that, at their best, words should wield the sensorial potency of images. The Horatian "ut pictura poesis" is very much alive in the ubiquitous analogies between paintbrush and tongue, paintbrush and pen, colors and words. Just as stories are commonly regarded as collections of *exempla* that put pictures in motion by threading them into a narrative, pictures are deemed to bring narratives to life by giving them a perceptible shape. Thanks to a wealth of distinguished studies on the relationship between text and image, our understanding of their symbiosis has grown considerably (de Armas, *Writing* and *Quixotic*; Ledda; Gallego).

In bringing particular paintings and emblems to bear on Quevedo's writing, I do not mean to claim that there are implicit references to those specific artworks in his corpus. Rather, my intent is to integrate pictorial works—in terms of their thematic content or their form—in a larger reflection on the mental and social conception of the culture of display, so as to think about Quevedo's complex role within it. In that spirit, as we turn our attention to how the convergence between image and text is perpetuated in the interpersonal realm, we can begin by noting the direct relationship between the conscious elaboration of imagistically persuasive techniques present in sermon collections or preaching manuals, scenes of parishioners transfixed by an emphatically delivered homily, and introspective meditation programs. All of these venues are premised upon the idea that seeing is believing, that feeling is knowing. The extent to which mental life is consciously centered upon physical stimuli is eloquently summed up in the prologue to the *Adnotationes et meditationes in Evangelia,* an annotated and pictorially illustrated commentary of key Gospel episodes, by Saint Ignatius of Loyola's collaborator, Jerónimo Nadal. A literal realization of Loyola's spiritual program, Nadal's meditations harness inward contemplation concretely to particular figures and exegetical formulae: "Spend a whole day, even several days, with each image. Read the Annotation and Meditation points slowly. Meditate, contemplate, pray over the whole exercise" (102).

The philosophical and psychological principles underlying this doctrinal method of directing mind and body are equally operative outside of the catechetical sphere. Conduct manuals and political treatises attest to the fact that the vision of life as a sensorially motivated process of fashioning and self-fashioning is deeply entrenched in the secular realm as well. In a variety of different ways, advice books propose what is, at bottom, the same recipe for personal success and social order: the artful use of language and gesture to influence others, or, conversely, the endeavor to perfect oneself through mimicking the language and gesture of ideal social actors.

That an acute bodily awareness is pivotal to this enterprise finds reaffirmation in the current surge of studies on the body in early modernity (Hillman and Mazzio; Harvey; Kern Paster, Rowe, and Floyd-Wilson). Adopting what they refer to as an "interpretive literalism," several scholars analyze metaphorical representations of the body not as intertextual elaborations, but rather as direct references to somatic sensation (Hillman and Mazzio xx). Much is made of the epoch's increased awareness of physiology, considerable attention being lent to the connections between literary texts and anatomical treatises. Given the tenuous position of the scientific revolution in Spain, one would have to be careful about determining the applicability of some of these approaches—which focus a good deal on England—in the Spanish context. That said, their materialist grounding is useful here because it accentuates the cultural importance of the sensory world, which is certainly perceptible in Spain (García Santo-Tomás). The initiation of hospital reforms geared toward rationalizing protocols for treating the sick, for instance, attests to the fact that Spain was not impermeable to the mounting prominence of the body as a discrete individual mechanism warranting scientific explanation, a notion that had gained wide impulse with the 1543 publication of Vesalius's *De humani corporis fabrica* (Redondo 155). Also a testament to this is the key role given to medical authority in determining the daily care and diet of the king and his family (Redondo 117). However, such developments should not be dissociated from Tridentine religious and political discourses in which the protagonism of the physical body had a long-standing history. Sentient human experience had long been a central component of Catholic devotional practices, relatable, in turn, to Thomistic visions of the world as a text to be deciphered. Hence the renewed corporeal awareness brought about by the advancement of physiological knowledge is intimately fused with these traditional schemes in which the body is the palpable reflection of the soul as well as of divine providence.

In his introductory remarks to Juan de Palafox y Mendoza's *Historia real sagrada,* Father Andrés de Valencia notes a hermeneutical linkage between physical matter and divine order: "De suerte, que las palabras de Dios, por lo que tienen de claro, con los ojos se pueden vér, aunque sean palabras, porque son palabras de luz, cuyos rayos son los objetos de la vista" (qtd. in Palafox y Mendoza 282).[3] By articulating a relationship between the seen and the unseen, between words and images, between the divine and the mundane, by intertwining human materiality and transcendental scheme, such providential allegoresis provides an authoritative conceptual basis for political action. A core political trope, the conception of the king as portrait of God on earth, constituted a crucial mechanism for representing the earthly realization of godly design. Moreover, the accompanying notion that order is conserved through the propagation of example radiating out from the king's person further confirms the actuality of divine plan (Santa María 195).

Those who defend the supposed liberty afforded by impersonal or mechanized means of transmission have argued that such traditional body-centered schemes curtail independent subject formation. Elaborating upon the terms of this opposition between a premodern "order of the body" and a modern "order of texts," Harry Berger synthesizes some of its main assumptions:

> Thus we read about societies in which the bodily signs of gender, genealogy, and age provide the organizing categories of institutional life, so that, for example, economic and political roles are embedded in sexual, domestic, kinship, and lineage roles. [. . .] We characterize embeddedness as a totalizing effect produced by the tendency of the signifying body to expand into all available spaces until it permeates society, nature, the cosmos, and the gods with the resonance of its categories, imagery, and voice. Finally, we attribute to embeddedness an ideological import that derives from a specific signifying power of the body. [. . .] The signature of the body confers the appearance of inevitability, inalienability, and transcendent reality inscribed in it by "nature." "Nature" in return borrows those forms of being that the human body signifies: person, consciousness, presence, and self-presence. In a word (a Derridean word), both the communicative and semiotic powers of the body, both the performance community and the embedded cosmos, are logocentric. (147–48)

The late moderns would see themselves as liberated from this regressive "logocentrism" and would argue "that the universes of the various sciences were disembedded from the constraining symbolism of the perceptual world; that the technological expansion of sensory and labor power came about by freeing instruments and machines from the limits of the body and its tools, which also meant freeing them from its control" (Berger 148). And yet this argument, Berger goes on to show, is highly suspect because it ignores the power relations also operative in "disembedded" interpretive communities.

Furthermore, the body-centered theological schemes on which the culture of performance rests do not, of themselves, render finite the interpretive process. Thinking specifically about visual culture, André Lascombes remarks that images are a means not only of exerting power by imposing a given meaning, but also of questioning it (29). More generally, the shifting condition of textual interpretation is fully operative in the interactive social realm, as is illustrated in Margaret Greer's reflection on how the physical mise-en-scène of Calderonian drama plays a key role in generating a nuanced critical view of royal power (*The Play*).

In post-Tridentine culture, moreover, the practice of patristic exegesis promotes interpretive creativity insofar as the linkages between earthly particulars and divine universals in allegorical and anagogical commentary were subject to constant elaboration and reinterpretation. Already in his foundational theory of reading, Augustine fully recognizes the polysemic life of texts: "So what difficulty is it for me when these words [of Genesis] can be interpreted in various ways, provided only that the interpretations are true?" (*Confessions* 259). It would be naive to deny the extent to which ecclesiastical and political authorities use both the liberties and the overarching teleological claims inherent in this theory to their instrumental advantage, for instance, when they present the Habsburg monarch as direct descendent of the Davidic line and harbinger of messianic redemption. However, such propagandistic designs do not exert centrifugal force on all cultural productions. Diverging from the position that the antiguo régimen was impervious to progressive thinking, I emphasize the senses in which its discourses are permeated by a markedly pragmatic spirit, which promotes individual initiative (see Maravall 76–77, 92).

The prevalent idea of reading events and people like texts and the corollary principle of managing one's own conduct and body image so as to control the readings of others, conceptions that were at the root of *prudencia*—considered the foremost political and social virtue—presuppose a good deal of behavioral creativity. Indeed, the political appropriations of the sacramental "Word made flesh" reveal that this organic metaphor is variously adapted to secular needs. If there is a unifying feature shared by the anti-Machiavellian writers, it is their transformation of doctrinal theology in accord with the demands of pragmatic statesmanship and their related belief that good speech and gesture are of essential value to successful government. For all their overt repudiation of Machiavelli's conviction that one must use force and ingenuity to get the better of Fortuna, the Spanish ideologues of the late sixteenth and seventeenth centuries strongly advocated wily know-how and strategic image construction. There is, at this time, an almost universal recognition of the need for spontaneity and flexibility. As the Count-Duke of Olivares once said, echoing a view widely accepted by his contemporaries, "The first rule of all is to be for ever on the lookout for the unforeseen and accidental" (qtd. in Elliott, *The Count-Duke* 23). Such promotion of inventive practicality is an important step in the birth of the "detached" subject (Cascardi 80) of later modernity, of which the Baroque *discreto* is a precursor. Carefully calculating his course of action and controlling his speech, the courtier directs an observer's eye to society; although embedded in the world of spectacle, he maintains an analytic distance from it. In other words, the "logocentrism" or "symbolic constraints" that, according to Berger, have been attributed to performance-centered communities cannot be said to completely define Quevedo's epoch. In a milieu that prizes wily resourcefulness, social being comes to be conceived as a deliberately crafted construction, rather than as a natural extension of universal principles.

Along with the sensorially based models of imitative conditioning, alternative paradigms of social order and reform develop that do not center on corporeal presence, for example, the conception of politics as a science (Quijada and Bustamante; Viroli) and the emergence of economic theory (González de Cellorigo; Moncada). Evident in works such as Sancho de Moncada's *Restauración política de España,* which proposes that Spain's problems can be remedied by modifying the financial system and stimulating domestic manufacturing, and Baltasar Álamos de Barrientos's compendium of Tacitean dictums for political success (*Aforismos*) is the belief that society can benefit from a pragmatic rationality.

It is against these tendencies that Quevedo's cultural program is to be situated. Regarding emergent pragmatism as the epitome of social decay, Quevedo upholds the "order of the body" in the most radical sense; that is to say, he views it as incompatible with rationalized or nonmythical praxes. His recipes for Spain's ongoing political and social problems are steeped in categorically prerational conceptions of knowledge and communication. He thus promotes the deployment of forms of political symbolism that ensure, again as Berger has put it, "the appearance of inevitability, inalienability, and transcendent reality." Such power is, furthermore, linked, in no uncertain terms, to the illusion of direct presence. It is no coincidence that Quevedo's writings contain numerous representations of rhetorical performance, such as the Messiah preaching to his disciples, Renaissance statesmen swaying the multitude, poets or playwrights mesmerizing their audiences, and professional men of letters holding forth before their clients. On one level, the situational variety of the rhetorical contexts encompassed in his corpus—ancient and modern, sacred and secular, aesthetic and bureaucratic—attests to Quevedo's currency with the concrete function and impact of eloquence in early modern society. On another, however, his characterizations of verbal exchange, whether in his satires or in his doctrinal treatises, are, to a large extent, informed by a strong reaction against the compartmentalization of languages set in motion with the development of the state.

I am referring to emergent visions that involve a transition from a traditional order, in which life—political and social—is organized around moral and religious schemes, to a modern order, with its development of distinct forms of practical expertise. One can think of these as denoting a kind of discursive and epistemological fragmentation: notions of ideal good or divinely ordained principles are increasingly relegated to a ceremonial terrain, whereas the running of government is recognized as being dependent upon the application of discrete bodies of pragmatic or technical knowledge (economic, juridical, administrative, political), each having its own specific language and logic, independent from an encompassing mythical order. Quevedo aims to construct a forceful rhetoric to oppose such disciplinary divisions and to stem the growing gap between concrete action and divine authority. In investing word and gesture with great force, his doctrinal treatises reclaim the power of creative invention in the political realm. Far from being relegated to the sphere of pleasurable artifice, art here acquires a leading social and sacred role. Consistent with this, in his satires Quevedo expresses profound aversion toward the use of rhetorical artifice for purely secular exhibitionist purposes.

His royal advice books see political redemption as being entirely contingent upon the conservation of a strong performative *praesentia,* which restores centrifugal power to the act of transmission itself (again, Agamben, *The Man* 107). Quevedo thereby counters the growing role of technical or pragmatic languages in the administration of the state and, in the cultural realm, the orientation of aesthetic production away from political action. We note that those at both extremes of the linguistic spectrum, the technocrat and the *cultista* poet, are equally maligned in his satires.

In essence, then, Quevedo espouses a eucharistic definition of communication that, as I shall show, invites comparison with Hans Georg Gadamer's organic connection between language, spectacle, and the visual arts as "events of being" (116). The pertinence of the comparison becomes all the more evident when we take into account Gadamer's critique of the social dominance conceded by modernity to scientific thought and technological expertise and his use of Christian articulations of sacred experience in formulating a theory of knowledge that contests the Enlightenment claim to eliminate prejudice or prejudgment. At the same time, Quevedo's vision of synesthetic impact as an absolute political instrument clearly contrasts with Gadamer's stipulation that his ontological approach be used not for political domination, but rather for speculative philosophical investigation (Warnke). "My real concern was and is philosophic: not what we do or what we ought to do, but what happens to us over and above our wanting and doing" (Gadamer xviii).

Meanwhile, the sacramental bias of Quevedo's poetics evolves into a denunciation of political and social change. Epochal malaise takes shape in his satirical texts as a chaotic expansion of adulterated languages. The various kinds of rhetoric he lampoons are shown to be utterly disembodied formulae, that is, artificial fabrications devoid of any substantive grounding and diametrically opposed to a ritualistic scheme in which the word is an extension of a corporeal divine being. Walter Benjamin's view of the Baroque individual confronting an explosion of signs is applicable to Quevedo's nightmarish visions of the arbitrariness of contemporary semiotic systems. In the *Origin of German Tragic Drama,* the dilemma of the Baroque subject is, precisely, the epistemological confusion produced by a lapsed and ever fluctuating symbolic universe. According to Benjamin, the persistence of death figures in the *Trauerspiel* emblematizes the perceived tenuousness of the connection between the worldly and the divine realms. Gone, then, is the stability afforded by Renaissance schemes in which observed phenomenal reality is directly inscribed in divine teleologies. What is particularly useful for our purposes in Benjamin's formulation is that it sees epistemological tensions mirrored in the experiential and social planes. Similarly, Quevedo's attempts to confer meaning or to bemoan its absence are ciphered in an atomized social body in which people, human ties, and physical matter have become empty or replaceable signifiers (Wolin 68).

Legitimate communication being contingent upon direct contact, disembodied modes of rapport are taken as signs of the degradation of language's referential and social power. It would be simplistic to claim that, for Quevedo, "aura"—again, a Benjaminean term ("The Work")—literally resides only in the spoken word. Many a burlesque treatment of oral usage is to be found among his writings, while certain kinds of written language are eulogized. Hence it is more accurate to say that ideal language, spoken or written, is that which communicates its continuity with an executive source, whereas depraved language is that which ill conceals its nature as a merely conventional form. If paper and print are at times evoked as symbols of the breakdown of the relationship between rhetoric and action, it is because they epitomize a dissociation between author and audience, the stripping away of experiential density. There is in these instances an implicit causal link between lack of genuine signifying power and the boundless reproducibility of printed matter; indeed, the uncontrolled expansion of communication across large audiences is likened to social and cultural dismemberment. In this sense, we can compare Quevedo's preoccupation with modes of circulation to the concern felt by some today that the displacement of books and newspapers by infinite cyberspace means the end of substantive cultural exchange, the opening of a Pandora's box of free-floating uprooted meanings (Beaudrillard). Diverging from eulogies of writing and print as the ultimate vehicles of civilization, Quevedo is ever suspicious of their counterfeit nature.

In sum, as will become evident in the course of this analysis, our author fluctuates between extreme identification with the apparatus of cultural display and its subversive anatomization. In rejecting the negotiations undertaken by many of his contemporaries between body-centered ideals and alternative forms of knowledge and transmission, Quevedo sets himself apart from pacified forms of civic and aesthetic engagement that were instrumental to the birth of the modern subject.

Discussing the first part of Quevedo's two-volume royal advice book, *Política de Dios,* chapter 1 illustrates the connections between the spheres of sacred oratory, political ritual, and imperial iconography in Counter-Reformation Spain. It considers how the notion of art as a living enactment, which is thereby capable of a dynamic social and psychological influence over its audience, is ubiquitous in early modern culture. In keeping with this trend, I argue, Quevedo's political prose conceives of the practice of rulership as active symbolic representation, a conception that approaches Gadamer's eucharistic definition of perception. I contrast Quevedo's entirely thaumaturgical depiction of political power, which makes use of the tradition of the royal touch, with the vision of rulership present in other anti-Machiavellian royal advice books that separate the mythical function of the king from his mortal person. In doing so, I show that the degree of synthesis between Christological ritual and political practice depicted in the text is unorthodox for its own time: it violates core contractual principles on which the king's institutional legitimacy was traditionally founded.

Focusing on the second part of *Política de Dios,* chapter 2 considers Quevedo's use of the Passion of Christ as a central allegory of political authority. Situating Quevedo's emphasis on the suffering Christ and his intensified use of eucharistic metaphors in relation to devotional practices and processional sculpture, I contend that the political symbolism deployed in this later text continues to promote a body-centered notion of government. At the same time, I show that the display of the royal body bears a markedly different semiotic charge from that of part I. The *imitatio Christi* takes on a new meaning as the rigid corporeal codes of court protocol are displaced by a pathos-ridden political theater. The metaphor of the king's touch, on which royal communication is modeled in part I, develops into depictions of a prodded, beaten, and tormented king. I read such emphasis on bodily violence, in sociological terms, as a model of communication that runs counter to the "civilizing process" (pace Elias).

Any discussion of early modern political communication would be incomplete without mention of the republican rhetorical tradition that played such a formative role in Counter-Reformation oratory. Chapter 3 reads the representation of Cicero's death contained at the conclusion of *Marco Bruto*—a political manual organized as a commentary on Plutarch's *Life of Brutus*—as a reflection on the fate of the virtuous orator in the age of the bureaucratic state and the "paper king." I devote particular attention to the transition from the Quintilian ideal of the "vir bonus dicendi peritus" to a Senecan pointedness. Following contemporary trends, Quevedo abandons the model of the good citizen speaker in favor of the laconic wit. Paradoxically, however, he lays strong emphasis on the Tacitean distinction between useful and entertaining rhetoric, showing a pronounced bias against the autonomy of verbal invention from concrete political action. I highlight Quevedo's recalcitrant posture through contrast with other contemporary rhetorical theorists and ideologues who reconcile the domestication of arts and letters with Longinean ideals of excellence and preeminence. Divergently, in an attempt to reanimate verbal expression, Quevedo imbues the communicative act with an inordinate aggression that unsettles the civic practice of courtly composure.

Chapter 4 focuses on *La Hora de todos*, Quevedo's most important political satire, which serves as a framework to further think about the potential conflict between traditional conceptions of heroic eloquence and emergent early modern manifestations of statehood. I discuss Quevedo's apocalyptic representation of the general corruption of language in connection with an indictment of the paper culture. I argue that his sweeping denunciation of the linguistic conventions used by all manner of civil servants, men of letters, and poets as debased forms of deceit that bring about social and political collapse serves to magnify the cultural tensions that accompany the displacement of oratorical and performative ideals as exclusive models of societal organization. Approaching the subject of verbal and corporeal display within the sphere of the grotesque and the political pamphlet, my discussion of *La Hora de todos* illustrates how the conviction that social order depends on the possibility of preserving the exclusive power of mystifying forms of communication is a constant underlying premise across Quevedo's oeuvre. I contend that the satire imagines the large-scale operation of governmental norms and cultural conventions beyond the self-contained universality of the court as a kind of erratic mass commodification, which brings about a radical loss of authoritative *praesentia*, thereby shattering the organicity of the body politic. Contrasting the antithesis that Quevedo draws between expanding audiences and sacred presence with Thomas Hobbes's fusion of state machine and natural and divine bodies, and drawing on Benjamin's ("The Work") and Marshall McLuhan's theories on the sensorial effects of mechanized communication, I expound upon the clash between materialist and metaphysical schemes dramatized in *La Hora de todos*. I conclude that the flexibility of the allegorical process that allowed the emergent modern state to continue binding its temporal history to a teleological order is severely undercut; the very possibility of perpetuating a symbolic system capable of sustaining Tridentine Spain's social and political legitimacy is called into question.

1

CRAFTING ROYAL OMNIPOTENCE

Y tal vez se llama el poeta pintor y pintor el poeta.

—Francisco Pacheco, *El arte de la pintura*

FROM THE MYRIAD EMBLEMS of the immortalized planet king to those representing the ruler's death, from Titian's painting of a triumphal Philip II as Rex Sacerdos to Diego de Velázquez's portraits of a soberly dressed Philip IV, without regalia, images of kingship in early modern Spain vary greatly in their symbolic implications (figs. 1–5).[1] On the one hand, the ruler is aligned with cosmic forces, as exemplified in Andrés Mendo's depiction of regal power as a shining sun at the center of a globe surrounded by the circle of the zodiac (fig. 1). Included in Juan de Solórzano Pereira's *Emblemata regio politica,* Mendo's emblem is meant to illustrate the principle displayed in its inscription, "Sic Regat Rex Solvm, vt Sol Regit Polvm," that is, "Let the King Rule the Earth as the Sun Rules the Sky." Also evoking superhuman powers, Titian's painting invests royal might with sacramental as well as martial connotations (fig. 3). Made in celebration of Philip II's victory over Lepanto, the work shows the king standing before a bound and half-naked Turkish prisoner of war, who is seated in the lower foreground. Military triumph and Christian mission are intertwined as the victorious king, in priestly gesture, holds his infant son, Prince Ferdinand, above an altar, firmly fixing his gaze on the angel who reaches down from the sky to touch the baby's outstretched hand. Coexisting with such representations of eternal imperium are visions that accentuate the human condition of the ruler. In this spirit, the emblem included at the end of Saavedra Fajardo's *Empresas políticas* (originally titled *Idea de un principe politico christiano*) portrays a crown strewn on the ground beside a skull that sits on the ruins of a once palatial building (fig. 2). Less ominous, although every bit as solemn, are Velázquez's renderings of a darkly clad Philip IV (figs. 4–5). Whether or not one interprets the aging king's serious expression (fig. 5) as careworn melancholy

FIG 1. Andrés Mendo, emblem, "Sic Regat Rex Solvm, vt Sol Regit Polvm," in Solórzano Pereira's *Emblemata regio politica,* 1653. Biblioteca Nacional de España.

(see J. Brown 229), the kind of gravitas the portrait exudes—like that of the younger monarch (fig. 4)—is emphatically human. Far from the triumphalism implicit in renditions of boundless imperial dominance, such visions conceive of rulership as an onerous responsibility. Royal decorum from this perspective would be grounded in a stoic commitment to the burdensome obligations of government.

This view of kingship is pervasive in post-Tridentine mirrors of princes, a corpus of texts that will be of particular concern in this chapter. These Catholic royal advice books habitually urge the sovereign to temper authority with humility and compassion. Christian teaching is frequently punctuated by the gloomy reminder that the monarch's reign is only temporary: his life will come to an end and his body, like that of all mortals, will succumb to "Lvdibria Mortis" or "The Ravages of Death," as announced in the emblem that brings Saavedra Fajardo's treatise to a close (*Empresas* 1049). Such a notion would, in turn, be consistent with an aspect of Spanish royal protocol that often gave pause to foreign visitors. "Here," says a Welsh courtier come to Madrid in the 1620s, "it is not the style to

FIG 2. Emblem, "Lvdibria Mortis," in Saavedra Fajardo's *Idea de un principe politico christiano representada en cien empresas,* 1640. Artist unknown. Biblioteca Nacional de España.

claw and compliment with the king, or idolize him by 'Sacred Sovereign' and 'Most Excellent Majesty.' But the Spaniard, when he petitions to his King, gives him no other character but 'Sir,' and so relating his business, at the end doth ask and demand justice of him" (qtd. in Stradling 14). On the other hand, in the late sixteenth and the first half of the seventeenth centuries, there is a particularly strong investment in sacralizing monarchy, prompted in part by the rise of pragmatically oriented reason-of-state theories that drew attention to the superlative political instrumentality of theocratic myth (Feros, "'Sacred'"). But, even though in the propagandistic sphere the divine stature of the monarch is commonly underscored (Feros, *Kingship* 78), outside this sphere the imprint of contractual theories of government and of classical and Christian ethical discourses is still strong. Significantly, as Alban Forcione has shown, in their portrayals of "unrobed" humanized kings, some of the leading *comedias* of the period provide elaborate challenges to the concept of the heroic ruler formulated in official panegyrics (*Majesty*).

FIG 3. Titian, *King Philip II Offering His Son, Prince Ferdinand, to God After the Victory of Lepanto,* 1573–75. Museo del Prado, Madrid. Photo: Erich Lessing / Art Resource, New York.

Diverging from this tendency, like the reason-of-state theoreticians and the artists who contribute to the construction of a godly ruler, Quevedo brings the notion of the deified royal body to new heights. Appropriating the figure of the sacred Defensor Fidei in the domain of political education, his most important treatise, a mirror of princes titled *Política de Dios: Govierno de Christo,* contrasts starkly with other representatives of the genre. Rather

FIG 4. Diego de Velázquez, *Portrait of Philip IV as a Young Man,* 1628. Museo del Prado, Madrid. Photo: Scala / Art Resource, New York.

FIG 5. Diego de Velázquez, *King Philip IV of Spain*, 1655–60. Museo del Prado, Madrid. Photo: Erich Lessing / Art Resource, New York.

than offering moral guidance, the treatise develops a theory of communication that fuses religion and power in a manner that was extreme even for its own epoch, transgressing, as it did, the confines of the *humilitas* that was considered essential to political legitimacy.

If, in the realm of royal etiquette, the king's remoteness becomes one of the signs of his divinity (Elliott, "The Court" 154), in the terrain of executive decision making, his influence has become eclipsed by a growing state apparatus. With the rise of the favorite and of a formalized and bureaucratized system of government, the authority of the king is transmitted in an increasingly indirect manner. As John H. Elliott once put it, with the passage from the warrior king Charles V to the sedentary Philip II, "the Spanish Empire [. . .] passed out of the age of the conquistador into the age of the Civil Servant" (*Imperial* 170). It had become common knowledge that "government by paper" was replacing government by "spoken word" (Elliott, *Imperial* 170), a transition that many looked upon with distrust. The mocking label of "rey papelero" (Bouza, *Del escribano* 76), coined for Philip II, reflects a popular bias against the establishment of an impersonal government machine that rests upon set administrative procedures. Fully symptomatic of such bias is Quevedo's insistence on the unique and irreplaceable powers of the sovereign's word and presence, which will become evident in the pages to come.[2]

It is important to qualify the extent to which one can speak of a modern Spanish state. As Henry Kamen affirms, it is not until the reign of the Bourbons that the process of national unification initiated by the Catholic monarchs becomes an institutional reality (*Golden Age* 21–22). Moreover, as Elliott remarks, in seventeenth-century Spain, the concept of the state as an abstract entity operating apart from particular human or divine will is still somewhat alien to a people who conceive of political order in highly personalized terms, as based on a substantive connection between king and kingdom (*The Count-Duke* 182). But there are several respects in which the foundations of a modern state are in place. Although the word "state" is not commonly used, "reason of state" is already a well-established expression, even in the most doctrinaire of political treatises. The legacy of Giovanni Botero had definitively made its mark on the anti-Machiavellian ideologues. Even ethically minded royal mirrors took into account the demands of realpolitik (Mártir Rizo 97; Rivadeneira 525; Robbins 102).

Beyond the purview of political theory, the development of several forms of applied knowledge specific to pragmatic political or organizational goals is evident in a variety of settings, from the rise of the professional *letrado* to the institutionalization of juridical practices (Thompson; Kagan; Fayard), to the Crown's interest in the systematization of geographical and social information—the promotion of map drawing and population surveys, for example—to the development of economic analysis (Burke, *A Social History*; Quijada and Bustamante; Pérez 43). In stark contrast with those who blame the decline of Spain on the corruption of manners, writers like Martín González de Cellorigo offer empirical diagnoses of and remedies for the nation's financial and political ills. In his *Restauración política de España,* Sancho de Moncada, for one, proposes to cure Spain with the precision of a doctor. Although it is true that such propositions were often received with little enthusiasm in a world that had not altogether discarded its belief in the reformatory powers of noble virtue, the need for pragmatic know-how was generally accepted.

Keenly aware of the potential conflict between the emergence of the modern state and the survival of the heroic king, Quevedo, who must himself be considered an architect of Habsburg political symbolism, depicts an absolutist monarch who is at once a supreme embodiment of Christocentric traditions and a consummate statesman, a pious ruler and an expert administrator. In short, he propounds a powerful myth that invests the age of paper with the glory of epic ideals, by the same token, stressing the continued relevance of the cultic dimensions of kingship in an era of mediating political machines.

Written during the reign of Philip III, dedicated upon his death in 1621 to the young Philip IV and his favorite, the Count-Duke of Olivares, and extensively revised in 1626, part I of *Política de Dios* provides the new regime with a most timely icon.[3] The austere Christian king depicted by Quevedo is very much attuned to the sobriety of the Olivarian program, which attempts to change the climate of liberal patronage that had marked the Duke of Lerma's government (Olivares 246). Famous for his willingness to curtail customary noble privileges for the sake of fiscal responsibility, Olivares consciously differentiates himself from his predecessor, who spent wantonly to promote courtly clientage. Whereas Lerma distracted his king from the cares of state by drawing him to mundane enjoyments, Olivares endeavors to impress upon Philip IV the weighty obligations of good rulership.[4] His stoic mindset is well represented in Quevedo's call for the king's absolute commitment to duty. Throughout *Política de Dios,* Quevedo sententiously reaffirms the need for superlative dedication. Among the first mentions is made in the preface that he addresses "a Don Felipe, Quarto Rey, nuestro señor" (*Política* 40). He who has inherited the title of Monarch, says Quevedo, quoting the late antique bishop Synesius, "ha de tomar todo trabajo, ha de apartar de si toda pereza, darse poco al sueño, mucho a los cuidados, si quiere ser digno del nombre de Emperador" (*Política* 41). The towering monarch represented in the pages that follow would be in perfect consonance with the count-duke's intention to "'re-Catholicize' the image, policies, and ideological foundations of the monarchy" (Feros, "'Sacred'" 80).

In projecting his own persona as royal adviser, Quevedo explicitly differentiates himself both from writers who have drawn their political lessons from pagan antiquity and from those who have deliberately misrepresented the truth by obsequiously flattering the king in order to curry favor.

By contrast, he contends, his intent in writing is to closely adhere to Christ's words and actions: "Os hago, señor, estos abreuiados apuntamientos, sin apartarme de las acciones y palabras de Christo; procurando ajustarme quanto es licito a mi ignorancia, con el Texto de los Euangelistas" (*Política* 40). Worthy of note here, aside from his pretended modesty, is Quevedo's proclaimed faithfulness to the Gospels.[5] What he alleges to be a literal application of Christ's teachings is, of course, a most creative appropriation that transforms Christ's apostolate into the epitome of successful rulership. What we find in the pages of *Política de Dios* is not a concrete course of political action, nor a systematically argued code of ethics, but rather a series of iconic lessons on the projection of power, which reflect the overarching definition of leadership as the effective deployment of symbols (Marin 6).

Each chapter of the work makes use of scenes from the life of Christ to illustrate the facet of royal comportment specified in the epigraph. For the most part cited from one or more of the Gospels, the chapter epigraphs are often mottoes relating to the control of the king over his ministers and subjects. Representative of their general tenor would be the one at the beginning of chapter 22, which is a quotation from Matthew 4: "Al Rey que se retira de todos, el mal ministro le tienta, no le consulta" (qtd. in Quevedo, *Política* 120). Equally emphatic about the need for royal shrewdness is the quotation from Matthew 16, introducing chapter 12: "Conuiene que el Rey pregunte lo que dizen del, y lo sepa de los que le assisten, y lo que ellos dizen, y que haga grandes mercedes al que fuere primer criado, y le supiere conocer mejor por quien es" (qtd. in Quevedo, *Política* 85). The repeated references to the momentous dangers lurking around the king are accompanied by triumphal assertions of his might. Although mention is made of Christ's betrayal, imprisonment, and Crucifixion, major emphasis falls on his successes. The selection of episodes from Christ's life is in itself indicative of this: his hallowed birth and adoration by the Magi, the miracle at Cana, the scene where he feels a humble woman's touch through the throng of his followers, his anointment by Mary (sister of Lazarus), his healing of the sick with the strength of his words, his expulsion of the merchants from the temple, his subtle disciplining of his disciples, and his prevailing over Satan's temptation in the desert. Informed by the traditions of royal spectacle, theocratic iconography, religious oratory, and courtly discretion, Quevedo's rereading of these episodes renders Christ as epiphanic vision and magisterial actor.

In recent years, Roger Chartier and Fernando Bouza have argued for the importance of considering the forms of cultural transmission (manuscripts, print, oral communication) as a crucial component of the meaning of texts.

Veering away from analyses based solely on internal thematic or formal considerations, these scholars have developed a more encompassing treatment of cultural productions by attending to their existence as social and material practices. Whereas historians of early modern Spain have clearly advanced a precise understanding of the social and institutional practices constituting cultural life, as shown, for instance, by recent scholarship on intellectual elites and letrados (Quijada and Bustamante; Fernández), in the fields of literary and cultural studies there is still much work to be done on how the emergence of professional technologies arising with the centralized state is processed by the political imagination. The issue is an important one since the establishment of professional expertise divorced from exceptional virtue and distinguished lineage and the mediated nature of communication by written document necessarily affect cultural production as a whole. It is noteworthy, for instance, that the comedia abounds in examples of monarchs who intervene directly in the lives of their people, reflecting a nostalgia for feudal ideals that were in many respects no longer applicable. In effect, outsiders at the Spanish court were struck by how withdrawn the Habsburgs were.

In contrast to their French and English counterparts, Spanish monarchs scarcely made public appearances and, within the confines of their palaces, subjects were seldom granted immediate contact with them (Kléber Monod 135). If the elusiveness of the king could serve as a way to impress his grandeur on the public imagination (Elliott, "The Court" 154), there was also a generalized distrust of the government machine, a fear that the role of the royal body was becoming all too abstract. Stemming the gap between conventional ceremony and personal agency, Quevedo consolidates the loftiness of the global emperor with the active leadership of the feudal king. He cautions his royal reader on the perils of invisibility: "La presencia del Rey, es la mejor parte de lo que manda. [. . .] Rey que pelea y trabaja delante de los suyos, obligalos a ser valientes; el que los vè pelear, los multiplica, y de vno haze dos. Quien los manda pelear, y no los vè, esse los disculpa de lo que dexaren de hazer; fia toda su honra a la fortuna, no se puede quexar sino de si solo" (*Política* 62). Accordingly, his Christ king is at once a magnificent icon of cosmic stature and a dynamic leader, an archetypal figure and a living corporeal presence.

Carmen Peraita and William Clamurro have both contributed in significant ways to the discussion of how Quevedo's treatise constructs political authority. Clamurro's analysis of its use of biblical text (*Language*), Peraita's commentary on its connection to the sermon ("La oreja") and her earlier work on its reflection of court politics (*Quevedo* and "From Plutarch's Glossator") have fittingly turned our thoughts to the question of the praxis of power and away from approaches that situate the text solely within the parameters of political theory. Where the relationship of the treatise to classical political ethics is undeniable, the central concern of the work is clearly the effective imposition of monarchical authority, as Clamurro and Peraita well demonstrate. Still in need of elucidation, however, is the sense in which the work is embedded in the rhetorical, pictorial, and ceremonial programs of the Habsburg state.

The question of how *Política de Dios* relates to these programs is significant: it leads us to consider the perceived change in the nature of political communication to which Quevedo is responding. Together with the "division of the labour of domination," as Pierre Bourdieu ("From the King's House" 42) defines the modernization of government, we witness a division between the performative or the ceremonial realm and the realm of political action. Quevedo challenges this trend by endowing regal decorum with a sensorial immediacy that creates the illusion of active rulership.

Louis Marin's work on the royal image, Chartier points out, teaches us a valuable lesson by articulating the relationship of "las modalidades de la exhibición del ser social o del poder político con las representaciones mentales—en el sentido de las representaciones colectivas de Mauss y Durkheim—que conceden o rechazan credibilidad y crédito a los signos visibles, a las formas teatralizadas, que deben hacer reconocer como tal al poder, ya sea soberano o social" (*Entre poder* 79). *Política de Dios* stands as a particularly revealing instance of the many ways in which physical gesture, social convention, artistic representation, and conceptual discourse are inextricably bound. In direct opposition to a Platonic bias against the compromising of absolute revealed truth by the interference of unstable appearances, Quevedo sees political order as being utterly dependent on the calculated fashioning of word and body. Political philosophy and praxis are captured in the protean "exhibición del ser social," as Chartier has put it. The communicative power of this social being radiates from his bodily presence, a conception that rests as much on the notion that life is spectacle as on the notion that spectacle is an inalienable form of human existence. That is to say, curial etiquette acquires the emotional potency of sacred ritual.

"The process of eradicating violence, whose manipulation is in theory taken over by the absolute state," reasons Chartier, "makes possible the exercise of a political domination based on the ostentation of symbolic forms and on the representation of the monarchical power, given to be seen and believed even in the absence of the king by signs of his sovereignty" (*On the Edge* 96). On the other hand, one must consider a growing awareness of the potential emptiness of the "signs of his sovereignty." Quevedo's emphasis on the direct interaction between king and subjects, I would contend, is an attempt to preserve the currency of the "order of the body."[6]

The kind of sensorial experience operative both in Quevedo's political prescriptions and in the rhetoric he himself uses calls to mind Gadamer's ontological hermeneutics. Viewing human perception as utterly embedded in cultural tradition, Gadamer explains the hermeneutic exercise, which he sees as central to all understanding, in terms of the thick relationship between spectator and work occurring in the plastic and the performing arts. Regarding the latter, the play acquires its full meaning through the spectator, and, conversely, the spectator finds his essential being in the play. This being is understood not as a kind of aesthetic subjectivity, but rather as an essence that is fully realized in the representation of the work. Alluding to the expressive powers of the religious play over its audience, Gadamer specifies that criteria of taste are not relevant here. That is, the spectator's reaction is to be characterized not as an appreciation for how well executed the piece is, but instead as a more immediate fusion with its totalizing presence. "Just as the ontological mode of aesthetic being is marked by parousia, absolute presence, and just as an artwork is nevertheless self-identical in every moment where it achieves such a presence, so also the absolute moment in which a spectator stands is both one of self-forgetfulness and of mediation with himself" (Gadamer 128). In other words, the work becomes contemporary with the mind of its receptor (Gadamer 108). Similarly, Quevedo's approximation to the Gospels obviates the historical, geographical, and cultural distances separating his own context from that of their original composition. Paul Ricoeur, it is well to remember, would deem the awareness of these distances essential in the recovery of past traditions (55–56). Contrary to the kind of analytic clarity that Ricoeur's interpretive model wishes to safeguard, Quevedo's appropriation of the Scriptures is not geared toward explanation but rather toward rhetorical exploitation. The very opposite of the humility he claims in the preface, his ambitious linguistic practice seeks to reproduce the overpowering effect of the Gospels. His channeling of Holy Writ mirrors his ideal king's fusion with divine being: both, in other words, play a key role in the continued dissemination of a sacralizing corporeal presence.

Examining Quevedo's messianic rhetoric through the lens of Gadamerian hermeneutics alerts us to the radical historical self-consciousness of Quevedean aesthetics. Manifest in his political treatises is an ongoing attempt to collapse the boundaries between art and life, that is, to transcend the condition of culture as a rule-based and learned set of conventions. Although Gadamer points to the seventeenth century as a time still untouched by an autonomously defined aesthetic, a time when the theological paradigm conflating life and art continues to be conceived as the exclusive mode of communication, judging from the cultural tensions of the period, it is more accurate to say that the life-art fusion shows certain fractures. Just as critiques of print are founded on the notion that it is an inauthentic cultural medium, the prolonged polemic between *culteranos* and *conceptistas* brings to the fore the artificiality of stylistic conventions. Although by far predating the concept of the "natural sublime" (Soufas 304) that would so inform romanticism, the early moderns were clearly aware of the fabricated nature of culture and of the problems this presented. An extreme testament to their awareness would be the deliberateness with which Quevedo aims to erect organic models of artistic being and his resistance to alternative forms of social organization. Whereas Gadamer regards ontological transmission as inevitable—that which, as cited in my introduction, "happens to us over and above our wanting and doing" (xviii)—Quevedo is centrally concerned about its loss.

His aesthetic program can effectively be understood as an attempt to conserve the "aura" of cultural practices—to use the term employed by Walter Benjamin to describe the heightened sensorial state elicited by the direct experience of art before the atomizing effects of modern mechanical reproduction ("The Work" 223). Granted that the establishment of print in the early modern era did not signify as drastic a change in the relationship between culture and society as did the introduction of photography and other industrialized modes of mass communication in the nineteenth century. Nevertheless, the framework set up by the German critic is useful to us in the sense that, in the seventeenth century, there is a palpable unease about how the change in the material means of relaying meaning affects the social value of culture. True, at one level, in this period the living word, the painted or engraved image and written or printed texts are seen as intimately related modes of communication; furthermore, the notion of writing and painting as sister arts is linked to the fact that both function as means of inducing direct emotional responses in the audience (Bouza, *Imagen* 22 and *Communication* 8). However, there are signs that the organicity of the cultural apparatus is being called into question; indeed, the denunciation of useless books, of clumsy typesetters, and ignorant readers makes itself quite loudly heard (Bouza, *Communication* 12).

To further foreground the sense in which Quevedo's oeuvre is responding to these issues—by preserving the political and social efficacy of the "parole" (Ong, *Orality*), that is, the performative manifestations of verbal expression—I shall discuss its approximation to the ubiquitous metaphor of the world as a stage, making more explicit how *Política de Dios* elaborates a form of political communication that captures the magical nature of ritual.

The Great Theater of the Court

The conception of the world as a stage can be regarded as the fundamental organizing principle of the Habsburg *monarchia universalis*. It has become commonplace among historians of early modern Europe to study the palace and adjacent urban life as a locus of display, its material culture designed to impress upon its audience the image of a formidable otherworldly power. The imposing buildings of the Spanish Habsburgs, the paintings, sculptures, and tapestries that adorn their halls, and the ceremonies and plays that take place in them all contribute to endowing politics with transcendental significance. In the space of the palace and under the aegis of the king, at once "the principal actor" of this "magnificent theater" and its chief patron, all manner of artworks converge (Brown and Elliott 31). Paintings reproduce motifs often found in emblems whose dictums are elaborated in fictional and nonfictional writings and acted out in plays and social ceremonies. Thus, in a certain respect, curial society functions within a semiotic continuum in which life and artifice come together in the generation of what Jonathan Brown and John H. Elliott call a "language of glory" (147). The life of the king is, in great measure, orchestrated according to the demands of his role as a mythical figurehead. The daily rituals performed by him and his retinue—the *levers* and *couchers,* the solemn meals, the set poses and responses at public audiences—are all symptomatic of the mythical constitution of palace life (Apostolidès, *Le roi-machine* 51).

The prolific scholarship on the significance of the early modern city, palace, public festival, and court ritual as a system of political communication provides productive analytic paradigms that have not yet been sufficiently exploited in the study of early modern Spanish mirrors of princes. The few studies dedicated to this corpus tend to approach the works in connection with political theory debates, with scant regard for their connection to the state's apparatus of political communication.[7] Given that pragmatic thought and symbolic constructs do not operate in isolation from one another, it makes little sense to separate political theory and cultural practice. Works like Brown and Elliott's study of the Buen Retiro Palace, Jean-Marie Apostolidès's (*Le roi-machine*) and Peter Burke's (*The Fabrication*) pieces on the construction of monarchical image in ancien régime France, Bouza's book on the propaganda apparatus under Philip II (*Imagen*), Antonio Feros's article on Catholic monarchical representation in the age of Velázquez ("'Sacred'"), and the anthology of early modern court and civic spectacle descriptions by J. R. Mulryne, Helen Watanabe-O'Kelly, and Margaret Shewring lead us to examine the early modern political theater as a large-scale project aimed at molding the public imagination or, in the words of Clifford Geertz, at inducing "powerful, pervasive and long-lasting moods and motivations" (206).

As implied previously, the actual power of the great theater of the court over the "moods and motivations" of its subjects was by no means boundless. Among the most famous voices raised against the vanity of court life, Antonio de Guevara explicitly terms it impious: "Ésta es, pues, la profesión que los cortesanos hacen, ésta es la regla que en su religión tienen, a la cual no llamaré yo religión sino confusión, no orden sino desorden, no monasterio sino infierno, no frailes sino orates, no regulares sino irregulares, no rezadores sino murmuradores, no monjes del yermo sino hombres del mundo" (*Menosprecio* 233). The sacrality of royal ceremony is undercut through references to the degraded backdrop against which it takes place: "No me negarán los cortesanos que a la mañana, cuando van a palacio, en el espacio que hay del rey se vestir hasta oír misa, no se pongan a contar unos a otros lo que aquella noche han jugado, lo que han murmurado, las compañías que han tenido, las hermosas que han visto y aun las cortesanas que han engañado" (Guevara, *Menosprecio* 245–46). Present in much of the grievance literature of the time, such awareness of the discontinuity between the symbolic apparatus erected by royal propagandists and the urbane realities of the political machine suggests that, as Elliott has cautioned, where enormous resources are devoted to the demands of *reputación* in the Habsburg era, we must not take the intent of the designers of royal myth as evidence of their effect on the public ("The Court" 163).[8]

Consummate rhetorician that he is, Quevedo takes into account the difficulties of capturing the hearts and minds of the audience as he crafts his political performance. He promotes Christocentric cult as a solution to the needs of the times, blending together the Messiah, the courtier, and the civil servant; he quite deliberately addresses and dissipates the perceived disparities between secular and theocratic aspects of rulership, transforming the administrative and courtly realms through the aura of ritual experience:

> Señor es muy necessario, que los Reyes tienten y prueuen la integridad, el valor, la justificacion de sus ministros para enseñarlos, y conocer lo que pueden dissimular; quanto mas Christo facilita el negocio, con mayor teson le impossibilitan los Apostoles. Mala acogida hallan necessidades agenas en otro pecho que el de Christo; cosa que deue tener cuidados, y desvelados a los Reyes. Oiga V. Magestad, y lea cautelosamente lo que le propusieren en fauor de los que le siruen, los que le parlan. Assi diferencio yo al que con las armas, o con letras, o con la hazienda, y la persona sirue a V. Magestad, de los que tienen por oficio el hablar destos desde su aposento, y que ponen la judicatura de sus seruicios y trabajos en el aluedrio de su pluma. ¡Gran cosa, Señor, que valga mas sin comparacion hablar de los valientes, y escriuir de los virtuosos, y a vezes perseguirlos, que ser virtuosos ni valientes, ni doctos! ¡Que sea merito nombrallos, y que no lo sea hazerse nombrar! Enfermedad es, que si no se remedia, serà mortal en la mejor parte de la vida de la Republica, que es en la honra, donde està la estimacion. Al buen Rey la porfia de consulta sin piedad en necessidades grandes de sus vassallos, o criados, o benemeritos, en lugar de enflaquezerle, o mudarle de proposito, o enuilecerle el coraçon, le ha de obligar a hazer milagros, como hizo Christo este dia. (Quevedo, *Política* 66)

The "miracle" referred to here is Christ's power to command in adverse circumstances; even the desert and the dried-up fig tree give nourishment when so ordered by God or Christ, adds Quevedo. Such must be the king's power vis-à-vis even the less loyal of his subjects. This lengthy passage and the added specification vividly illustrate how Quevedo turns mundane government into the politics of God. Switching, in the space of a sentence, from the king's careful examination of official proposals—both written and spoken—to Christ's devotion to his ministry, from the king's psychological scrutiny of his subjects' loyalties to Christ's assiduous control of his flock, Quevedo defines the courtier bureaucrat in the image of the Rex Sacerdos. Otherwise said, *Política de Dios* subsumes the particular tasks of rulership within a mystical plane: the person of the king, the body of Christ, and the authority of God are one. Social and political conventions are thereby made synchronic with biblical time. And it is the very illusion of synchronicity that constitutes their executive power. In this scheme, the monarch's body, as physical incarnation of might, acquires a supreme preeminence.

Rex Sacerdos

Toute la grandeur & tout le bon-heur d'vn Prince consistent à faire par ses vertus vne image visible de la divinité invisible.

—Nicolas Caussin, *La Cour sainte*

The artistic programs commissioned under Philip II bring together, with increasing sophistication, the traditions of pagan cult and those of Christian theocracy (Tanner 148–49), as is, for instance, attested to by the construction of the vast Escorial palace-monastery-library complex, the most important building project of his reign. Classical and Judeo-Christian myth converge in a structure that is evocative at once of Solomon's temple, Olympian monument, and Christian sanctuary. Representations of Philip II, like those of his successors, include figures in military garb, holding sword and globe, reminiscent of Roman emperors; others associate the Habsburg monarchs with Jove and Apollo, still others connecting them to the genealogical line of Clovis, who in turn was held to be directly related to Old Testament kings.[9] An analogous Christianization of classical and Jewish traditions is well exemplified in one of Hortensio Paravicino's funerary sermons for Philip III. "Pero el verdadero hijo de Abraham, la copia de David cristiana, el fénix de la piedad, religioso Filipo Tercero, no sólo se levantará, ave nueva y solar, del mármol donde selló la fe los despojos de la parte o porción mortal temporalmente; no sólo será estrella que en perpetuas eternidades manche hermosamente de luz la parte que le toca del cielo; sol y ejemplo será de singulares virtudes a la tierra" (195).

It is true that, since the reign of Philip II, the identification between king and Christ had taken on a notable figural importance: a salient example would be the use of the Cross, underlined by "IHS," standing for "In Hoc Signo Vinces" (Tanner 202), as a Habsburg symbol. But Quevedo infuses new life into the idea of the king as *corpus mysticum* by illustrating its direct relevance to the sphere of concrete political action. In *Política de Dios* the pious king is clearly identified with biblical typologies: he is the sacrificial lamb, the temple, and at the same time the sun, the stars, the light of redemption. In the opening pages, Quevedo emphasizes Christ's position as unifying figure of a temporal continuum that links Old Testament and contemporary times.

Reiterating established apocalyptic visions, Quevedo cites Talmudic allusions to the Messiah who will liberate the Jews from the Romans, "Quòd Rex Messias iam natus est in fine secundi templi" (qtd. in *Política* 48), and goes on to affirm his fulfillment of Hebrew prophecy: Jesus reigns as father of "toda Israël [. . .] del futuro siglo" (qtd. in *Política* 48), as "hijo de Dauid [. . .] el Real Profeta, el santo Rey" (*Política* 49). Quevedo stresses Christ's role as universally acclaimed king: "Ni los Profetas, ni los Rabies incredulos, no echan menos la riqueza del Reyno temporal para llamarle Rey. Y siendo esto assi, le vieron exercer juridicion ciuil y criminal" (*Política* 48). Supreme in his miraculous apostolate, "militò con las palabras. Preso respondio con el silencio. Crucificado reynò en los oprobios. Muerto executoriò el vassallage que le deuian el Sol y la Luna, y vencio la muerte" (*Política* 48). We are reminded of J. G. A. Pocock's characterization of Machiavelli's prince, who must accomplish "a task beyond normal human powers," which demands "more than normal *virtù*; we must not say that divine inspiration is being lowered to the level of realpolitik without adding that realpolitik is being raised to the level of divine inspiration" (171).[10] Understanding politics from the parameters of rhetorical and ritual conquest, *Política de Dios* is emphatic in its assertion that the success of the king's reign—his ability to conserve order, to put it in Machiavellian terms—depends upon his capacity to imitate Christ with convincing allure.

Quevedo does much more than simply identify the king with emblematic encomiastic imagery. His political prescriptions constitute an attempt to exceed the power of panegyrical artworks; indeed, his pronounced concern with the king's active appropriation of these symbols is palpable throughout *Política de Dios*. The sententious tone of the work and its reiteration of the dangers besieging the ruler highlight the urgent need for the monarch to exert an extraordinary communicative power over his audience. Quevedo represents Christ's dialogues with his followers as specific examples of how this might be achieved. Preserving the magical charismatic character attributed by Max Weber to the early prophet, he posits these versions of the imitatio Christi not as allegorical constructions, but rather as vital forms of sacred experience.

The Experience of the Sacred: Beyond Explanation

My speech and my proclamation were not with plausible words of wisdom, but with a demonstration of the Spirit and of power, so that your faith might rest not on human wisdom but on the power of God.

—1 Corinthians 2:4–5

Augustine was explicit about the importance of eloquence: if one wants to move an audience to action, it is not enough to "persuade people of the truth of what is being said," nor "to give delight by the style" (*On Christian* 119).[11] Rather, "when advocating something to be acted on, the Christian orator should [. . .] move them so as to conquer their minds" (Augustine, *On Christian* 119). In this passage, the word is upheld as much more than merely a vehicle of communication: it becomes a source of unquestioned communion.

The conventions of Christian rhetoric, we learn from Augustine's *Confessions,* are in large measure a negation of rhetoric as a merely pragmatic contrivance. Indeed, Augustine expresses his conversion to Christianity as a break with his past teaching of rhetoric, the form of oratory incorporated in the Roman state curriculum, which he decries as linguistic manipulation. Intended for the political elite and for the civil servant, Roman rhetorical education centers on teaching the speaker how to ingeniously model tropes through a series of set techniques, the main goal being to succeed in persuading the audience of any given premise. It would be naive to take literally Augustine's renunciation of this conception of rhetoric: his own preaching is squarely founded in the Roman tradition, and much of the subsequent history of Christian oratory bears witness to its debt to Aristotelian and Ciceronian principles. However, it would be equally wrong to utterly dismiss Augustine's claim. After all, it does alert us to one significant difference in intent: in contrast with the classical orator, the Christian preacher aspires to an essential concurrence between language and extralinguistic truth. The task of biblical exegesis would be, at its best, a reenactment of the executive power of God's word (King 247). Thus, even though the notion that epideictic oratory could induce the audience to virtue was well entrenched in the classical world (Vickers 57), the imperative that it be understood as an emanation of revealed truth is a uniquely Christian proposition. Furthermore, the insistence on the actual reproduction of divinity is inevitably tied to the strict divide between the sacred and the profane world espoused by Christian doctrine, a divide that ultimately renders paradoxical the claim to direct contact with God.

In early modern Europe, where religious and political indoctrination go hand in hand, Augustinian rhetorical ideals continue to be fully operative: preachers equate eloquence and divine revelation. In his long-winded defense of rhetoric, Fray Luis de Granada terms it a pillar of the Church and reminds his readers that the first interpreters of the Scriptures were all endowed with this God-given faculty. After all, Granada reasons, "á los hombres que no pueden hablar, ¡de cuán poco les sirve aquel ánimo celestial! Por tanto, si lo mejor que hubimos de los dioses es la palabra, ¿qué cosa hemos de reputar por mas digna de nuestro cultivo y aplicación?" (495). In praise of Saint John Chrysostom, he says, "Sus palabras son tan propias, y fluyen tan suavemente, que no puede haber cosa más tersa y dulce: sus sentencias son tan sabias, que parecen infundidas por Dios, no inventadas por ingenio humano" (495). As is also the case with Augustine, the invisibility of rhetorical contrivance is a central rhetorical requirement.

Whereas Aristotle directed the master rhetorician to strike a balance between logos, pathos, and ethos, the Baroque rhetors lay greater stress on ethos and pathos. The capable preacher, Granada stipulates, instigates his flock to see and feel the substance of his message "para que la vean y como que la miren" (519). The audience, he adds, will be swayed if the sermon exposes its argument "no sumaria y ligeramente, sino por extenso y con todos sus colores, de modo que poniéndolo delante de los ojos del que lo oye ó lo lee, como que le saca fuera de sí y lleva al teatro" (538). Thus what counts is not the structural coherence of the argument, but rather the way in which it is dressed or "colored." For this is what conditions the experience it will induce in its audience.

Such a belief in the virtual power of illusion is also a central premise of advice literature. In his manual *El héroe,* Gracián would, with characteristic pointedness, emphasize the generative influence of heroes, contending that they propagated themselves through example, rather than through siring children: "Son los varones eminentes textos animados de la reputación, de quienes debe el varón culto tomar lecciones de grandeza, repitiendo sus hechos y construyendo sus hazañas" (36). This notion of a chain of imitation as a vehicle for the dissemination of glory is at the core of the imitatio Christi evoked by a number of mirrors of princes.

Juan de Santa María's *Repvblica y policia christiana* affords us a representative example of the organic link between art and life. Through the very act of imitating God—of being his portrait—the king maintains the health of the body politic:

> Siendo el Rey [. . .] el anima, y coraçon del Reyno, y como otro Sol, que con su luz y mouimiento, da luz y salud al mundo: vn retrato de Dios en la tierra, y el que mas (siendo justo) se le parece, tiene precisa obligaciō de con su vida y exemplo, dar vida, y exemplificar su Reyno, cuerpo mistico de quien tambien el es cabeça; y la dependencia que tienen de la cabeça los miembros en el cuerpo humano, essa misma, o poca menos tienen los vassallos de sus Reyes, y si ella està sana y buena, lo estan todos los miēbros, si maleada, todos padecen en ella. (195)

Explaining social ideals in terms of the visual arts, Saavedra Fajardo stipulates that, at a young age, the prince should be surrounded by portraits and sculptures of great leaders as well as by teachers who imprint on him the spirit of true royalty:

> El maestro se copia en el discípulo, y deja en él un retrato y semejanza suya. Para este efeto constituyó Faraón por señor de su palaçio a Josef, el cual, enseñando a los príncipes, los sacase parecidos a sí mismo. [. . .]
> [. . .] De los primeros esbozos y delineamentos pende la perfeción de la pintura; así la buena educación de las impresiones en aquella tierna edad, antes que robusta, cobren fuerza los afectos y no se puedan vencer. (*Empresas* 197–98)

For this reason, the prince must not be exposed to grotesque images, for this might have a negative impact on his behavior and development: "Que no se le ofrezcan objetos espantosos que ofendan su imaginación, o mirados de soslayo le desconcierten los ojos" (Saavedra Fajardo, *Empresas* 201).

Whereas there are discrepancies regarding the manner of moving the audiences—with figures like Huarte de San Juan arguing for a more naturalized expression and figures like Paravicino or Granada acknowledging the role of ornamental flair—there is consensus on the need to involve all aspects of the senses: mind and body, eyes and ears. As demonstrated by one of the leading theorists of the conceit, metaphorical richness is directly equated with synesthetic interplay. "L'argvtia vocale," explains Emanuele Tesauro, "è vna sensibile Imagine dell'Archetipa: godendo ancora l'orecchio le sue pitture, che hanno il suono per colori, & per penello la lingua. Ma Imagine abozata più tosto che finita; doue l'ingegno intende, piu che la lingua non parla, & il concetto supplisce doue manca la voce" (17). Weaving together the topoi of eloquent painting and vivid speech, Tesauro upholds a language based on nuance and innuendo. Meaning, that is, lies in the act of communication itself, which involves the audience in a dynamic relationship with the text. Crucial to the dynamism of this relationship is the preservation of the mysteries of metaphorical language: the voice is quieted; the image is insinuated rather than finished. Gracián vindicated the polysemy of figurative language with equal enthusiasm, envisioning forms of perception beyond the grasp of conceptual clarity. "Poco fuera en la arquitectura asegurar firmeza, si no atendiera al ornato. ¿Que symmetría, en griega o en romana arquitectura, así lisonjea la vista, como el artificio primoroso suspende la inteligencia en este elegante epigrama del ingenioso Zárate a la Aurora?" (*Agudeza* 1:54). The intent here is not a philosophical challenge to the stability of the relationship between signifier and signified, but rather a quest for far-reaching rhetorical effect. The passage above comes as a further elaboration of a commentary on the superlative oratorical skill of Saint Francis Xavier, who, in India, conquered the wills of all those around him, to the point that his presence was felt all the way to Navarra, where a crucifix would sweat every time he suffered.

Such potency is also invoked as a fundamental standard in treatises on painting that likewise stress live interaction between artwork and audience, as has been well noted in the field of response theory (Freedberg; Stoichita). Widely cited in this context is the story of Apelles' patron, Alexander the Great, falling in love with the Venus that he had painted. As defined in Alberti's *De pictura*, observes Brian Vickers, painting "consists of an imitation of nature made with an eye to its impact on the spectator," a definition that holds true for much of the epoch's visual production; moreover, the same tasks are required of the painter as of the orator: "docere, delectare, movere" (Vickers 345).

It comes as no surprise, then, that in the prologue to *Política de Dios*, Father Lorenço vander Hammen commends Quevedo for portraying the king "con la mayor propriedad, mejores colores y pinzeles, que se pudieran hallar en la tierra" (qtd. in *Política* 36). In search of the ultimate mind-altering synthesis between human word and divine essence, Quevedo impresses upon his audience that his voice exists in continuity with the "Verbo Eterno" sent by God (*Política* 34). Similarly, the king's imitation of Christ is understood as his reproducing the semblance of the Messiah's miraculous being through well-conceived words and gestures. The king's authority, like Christ's, is founded on the perception of his expansive presence. In other words, it is not the application of determined laws that preserves order, but instead the illusion of the king's omnipresent aura. Once again, Quevedo stipulates that the communication of this aura must occur through living example: written instructions do not suffice. "Vna cosa es en los soldados obedecer ordenes, otra seguir el exemplo. Los vnos tienen por paga el sueldo, los otros la gloria. No puede vn Rey militar en todas partes personalmente, mas puede y deue embiar Generales, que manden con las obras, y no con la pluma" (*Política* 63).[12]

Throughout *Política de Dios*, the immediate nature of communication between Quevedo and his audience, as between the king and his subjects, is repeatedly evoked. From the initial remark, "Decienda el discurso a nosotros" (*Política* 43), with which he begins his homilies, to his continual citing of the rhetorical questions posed by Christ to his disciples, to his concluding exhortation that the king imitate Christ whom he hears "dar vozes [. . .] por la pluma de los Euangelistas" (*Política* 130), Quevedo creates a seamless unity with a sacred presence.

At the beginning of the 1626 edition of *Política de Dios,* Quevedo protests against the "Dotores sin lvz" who had gotten their hands on earlier copies of the treatise and criticized its handling of Christian doctrine. In his defense, he argues, "Juntè dotrina, que dispuse animosamente, no lo niego; tal priuilegio tiene el razonar de la persona de Christo nuestro Señor, que pone en libertad la más aherrojada lengua" (39). This characterization of the Messiah as a force that unlocks the tongue—which cannot fail to remind us of the Erasmian "Christus orator perfectissimus" (Fumaroli 148)—captures the nature of the work itself as an active illustration of the powers of sacred rhetoric. In the course of his defense against his critics, Quevedo cleverly develops the parallels between his writing and the empowering qualities of Christ's words: "Yo escriui sin ambicion, diez años callè con modestia, y oy no imprimo, sino restituyome a mi propio, y vengome de los agrauios de los que copian, y de los que imprimen" (*Política* 40). The conceit distinguishing the printed word from the living presence of our author is revealing: the idea that he does not write but, rather, conveys his very "self" is a clear indicator of the extent to which the persona of the hallowed orator shapes the form and content of his political doctrine.

That Quevedo explicitly differentiates his work from doctrinal exegesis is also amply significant: "Dexo las explicaciones Escolasticas, y expositivas al Tesoro de los Santos Padres, y a las questiones de los varones doctissimos, que en esto han escrito, antiguos, y modernos: yo solo trataré de buscar enseñança Politica, y Catolica" (*Política* 272).[13] Particularly revealing here is the opposition he draws between scholastic exposition and Catholic political lesson. That his text is a collection of homiletic *exempla* is perfectly consonant with its view of Christian politics as an "epideictic performance" (Marin 137). Quevedo repeatedly implies that political mastery is most readily obtainable from an unlearned, that is, direct, contact with the Gospels. He explicitly distinguishes the role of political adviser from that of the philosopher: political efficacy resides not in deciphering biblical allegory, but rather in reproducing its ineffability, a fact well noted by his official readers. In his "Aprovacion," the Jesuit Gabriel Castilla praises *Política de Dios* precisely for this reason, "porque no consiste en continuo estudio de Escritura, ni perpetua leccion de Santos y Doctores, sino en viueza de ingenio [. . .] que [. . .] causa nueuos resplandores, que admiran y espantan" (qtd. in *Política* 30). Meanwhile, vander Hammen exalts the author for looking to the "fuente viua y perenne" of the

Holy Scriptures and turning his back on "los charcos y arroyuelos" of Plato's and Aristotle's writings (qtd. in *Política* 33). At issue specifically here is the fact that classical political theory centers on the clear definition of principles, such as justice and the good. Politics, as Quevedo sees it, lies exclusively in the allusive powers of palpable form that overwhelm the audience. We approach the mystical realm described in San Juan de la Cruz's well-known *copla,* where contact with the sacred involves forms of perception antithetical to intelligible feeling and knowledge: "Y el espíritu dotado / de un entender no entendiendo / toda sciencia tracendiendo" (264). Here the worshiper gives up all control of his perceptions.

To bring about this level of self-renunciation in his audience, the king must strike a delicate balance. His physical presence must be ubiquitously tangible, but at the same time, his body must be, paradoxically, out of reach. As we shall see, it is through maintaining a supreme control of his own emotions that the king can succeed in impressing his subjects with the overwhelming sensation of his unfathomable being.

The Royal Touch: Beyond Law

To others I speak in parables, so that "looking they may not perceive, and listening they may not understand."

—Luke 8:10

Although Quevedo's ideal king does not speak in parables, the intent of his words and gestures is, like that of Christ's figurative speech, to mystify. Therein lies the secret of his rhetorical power, the condition of what Giorgio Agamben terms the "exception" of sovereignty: "The specification that the sovereign is '*at the same time* outside and inside the juridical order' is not insignificant: the sovereign, having the legal power to suspend the validity of the law, legally places himself outside the law" (*Homo Sacer* 15). Likewise, on Quevedo's political stage, the king is not a keeper of the law: rather he *is* himself the law, meaning that he can redefine its terms. His presence amounts to a suspension of the law, as a clearly stipulated body of rules. Order is thus maintained through the audience's exposure to his thaumaturgical words and gestures. As formulated in Augustine's rhetorical philosophy, "The fusion of obscurity with such eloquence in the salutary words of God was necessary in order that our minds could develop not just by making discoveries but also by undergoing exertion" (*On Christian* 106).

Whereas other mirrors of princes turn to a deliberative rhetoric to explain or justify the value of the principles of government endorsed, *Política de Dios* limits itself almost exclusively to the epideictic, proceeding by active exemplification (Peraita, *Quevedo* 99). In his *Tratado de la religion y virtudes que debe tener el príncipe cristiano,* Pedro de Rivadeneira, devotes a number of pages to discussing the reasons for which "la conservacion de la república depende de la paz de la Iglesia" (502). Numerous examples from Christian and pagan history are given to prove that religious division breeds instability, whereas religious unity guarantees a strong state. By contrast, Quevedo, who assumes that social order is irrefutably founded on faith, devotes himself entirely to representing its effects. Telling in this respect is the direct link he establishes between the ethos of courtly discretion and the teaching of Christ. Crucial to the royal actor's embodiment of godly authority, the control of gesture is expressed as a primordial duty: "Rey que con el fauor diferencia en publico vno de todos, para si ocasiona desprecio, para el priuado odio, y en todos embidia. Esto suele poder vna risa descuidada, vn mouer de ojos cuidadoso; no aguarda la malicia mas preciosas demonstraciones. Christo quando le dixeron estando enseñando a las gentes: 'Aqui estan tu madre y tus parientes,' respondio con seueridad, que parecia despego misteriosamente: 'Mi madre y mis parientes son los que hazen la voluntad de mi Padre que està en el cielo'" (Quevedo, *Política* 69). As is evident here, the exchanges between Christ and his followers are imposed as natural models for the interaction between the king and his subjects. Quevedo's own rhetoric thus serves to exemplify that Christ's words and gestures are the quintessence of political efficacy. Such is their seeming lack of contrivance that they appear inherently powerful.

In all of his pronouncements, the Messiah is portrayed as being in utter command of those around him. Never giving in to the imprudent requests of his disciples, he exposes their ignorance and his omniscience. To Jacob and John's request that they be seated next to him in glory, he responds with a string of disarming rhetorical questions: "¿Podeis beber mi caliz, y morir mi muerte? [. . .] ¿Podreis tener mis trabajos, y padecer mis ocupaciones? ¿hablar bien y mejor que de vos propio de los que me siruen mas? ¿Podreis solicitar el premio para el benemerito, y oluidaros del interes propio?" (Quevedo, *Política* 93). Such a response, says Quevedo, makes the disciples aware of the price of what they are demanding. The Messiah then punctuates his speech by reminding them that it is not up to him, but rather up to God to give such gifts: "No es de mi daroslo a vosotros" (qtd. in Quevedo, *Política* 94). Such apparent self-effacement is a supreme device for consolidating his unity with godly might.

Through the adoption of a messianic expression, Quevedo maintains the myth of absolute power. As Norbert Elias makes clear in his sociological study of court society, the "absolutist" king is bound within a composite network of relationships that must be maintained for the general preservation of order (*The Court*). He is as much dependent on his subjects as his subjects are on him for the securing of the social identities that give their lives collective meaning. There are also, of course, concrete material limitations on the king's power. True, during the reign of the Spanish Habsburgs, power is increasingly concentrated in the hands of the king and the favorite. As attested to by Lerma's and, most prominently, Olivares's terms in office, established conciliar structures are bypassed and royal policies expedited through spontaneously convened juntas (Elliott, *The Count-Duke*). However, it would be wrong to say that the executive had unlimited authority. The preeminence of regional *fueros* over royal sovereignty, the sporadic popular uprisings against royal government—for example, the revolts of the *comuneros* in 1520–21, the Moriscos in 1569, the Catalonians in 1640, the Portuguese in the 1640s and 1650s—as well as various protests against local, noble, and ecclesiastical authorities, make clear that the notion of checks and balances is very much alive among popular and elite sectors (Kamen, *Golden Age* 18–20). Although diminished, the *cortes* and councils do continue to function and, at least at a symbolic level, to affect royal initiative (Kamen, *Spain* 18–20).

A constitutionalist mindset is well represented in much of the political literature of the time. The emphatic rejection of tyranny, the notion that the king is a public servant who must govern within the law for the public good, and the view that he governs best in conjunction with wise ministers are all staple claims of early modern mirrors of princes, from Juan de Mariana's radical *De rege et regis institutione* (1598)—renowned for its defense of tyrannicide—to Saavedra Fajardo's absolutist *Empresas políticas* (1640). In short, beyond the patent ideological differences between anti-Machiavellians who identify with scholastic and Renaissance republican traditions and those endorsing the practice of absolutism, the notion of unlimited power is generally frowned upon. Quite indicative of the balance between royal prerogative and obligation defended by the Spanish Counter-Reformation thinkers is Santa María's assertion that the king's will is bound by constitutional, natural, and divine laws: "Este es el oficio de los buenos Reyes, honradamente seruir; porque en siendolo, no dependen sus acciones de sola la voluntad de sus personas, sino de las leyes y reglas que le dieron, y cōdiciones con que le acceptaron. Y quando falten a estas [. . .] no pueden faltar a las que le dio la ley natural y diuina, tan señora de los Reyes como de los vassallos" (19). Even Saavedra Fajardo, who sets much store by the king's ability to maintain his imperium, regards core classical virtues as indispensable; he says quite explicitly that the exhibition of power must be both tempered by mercy and guided by justice (*Empresas* 375; see also Mártir Rizo 31, 83). Linking justice specifically to established law, Saavedra Fajardo goes into a long excursus on why, in the course of history, republics developed written law codes: this was done to avoid the danger of depending solely on the opinion and judgment of the prince (*Empresas* 358). He further asserts that "no conviene apartarse de la ley, y que obre el poder lo que se puede conseguir con ella. En queriendo el príncipe proceder de hecho, pierden su fuerza las leyes" (*Empresas* 359). The tendency of modern scholars to interpret Spanish anti-Machiavellian treatises on kingship within the parameters of classical political thought is in this sense quite justified. Contrary to the excessive grounding of early modern English literary scholarship on Ernst Kantorowicz's *The King's Two Bodies,* as noted by Lorna Hutson (167), the influence of this study on early modern Hispanism has been somewhat less pronounced. It is not until fairly recently that scholars have begun to consider the sacramental aspects of Spanish kingship as they explore the symbolic foundations of political power (Lisón de Tolosana; Kléber Monod; Tanner; Feros, "'Sacred'"). Taking our cue from Hutson, we should bear in mind that the cultic conceptions of rulership to be found in ceremonial and pictorial programs are only one facet of Spanish political culture. As I have made clear, on a number of fronts, the Spaniards reject the idea of a deified king. The Spanish king does not, as do his English and French counterparts, wear a crown, nor is he anointed upon accession to the throne, nor is he thought of as literally having thaumaturgical powers.

Política de Dios stands apart from other exemplars of the genre in that the king's exceptionality is the basis for his authority. Keeping to the assumption that political order resides in the king's ability to mesmerize his audience, Quevedo adheres exclusively to a mythopoetic conception of rulership. The aim of his rhetoric is to arm the sovereign with a semblance of omnipotence. By imagining the royal distribution of goods in terms of the concession of godly grace, Quevedo obviates the relative power of the subjects, establishing a vast distance between the king and his ministers. The fact that the king is at times beholden to his subjects is negated: Christ's requests are defined as commands. The king alone is one with the divine source of power. Quevedo specifies that the sovereign "tiene Dicipulos, no tiene priuados que le descansen, [. . .] vino a redimir, no a ensoberuecer con vanidad ambiciosos, ni entremetidos" (*Política* 81). These disciples must learn that they are but shadows of his greatness.

Quevedo, in short, violates the boundaries between mundane rulership and divine immortality that the anti-Machiavellian tractarians had so carefully respected. In his scheme, the imitatio Christi means that the king himself exudes divinity. Moreover, allusions to his thaumaturgical faculties link Quevedo's king with archaic traditions of ruler worship. In one of the Gospel scenes recounted by Quevedo, Christ feels a woman's touch, even though he is surrounded by a throng of people:

> "Dezia entre si: Con solo tocar su vestido sere salua, y sintio en el cuerpo, que auia sanado de la plaga, y IESVS conociendo en si mismo la virtud que auia salido de si, buelto a la multitud dixo: ¿Quien tocò a mi, y a mis vestidos? y negandolo todos, Pedro, y los que con el estauan dixeron: Maestro las olas de la multitud, te bruman y afligen, y tu dizes, ¿quien me tocò? y dixo IESVS, alguno me tocò, porque yo conoci que salia de mì virtud."
>
> El buen Rey, Señor, ha de cuydar no solo de su Reyno, y de su familia, mas de su vestido, y de su sombra, y no ha de contentarse con tener este cuydado; ha de hazer, que los que le siruen y estan a su lado, y sus enemigos vean que le tiene. [. . .]
>
> Tocò la pobre muger la vestidura de Christo. El llegar a los Reyes, y a su ropa, basta a hazer dichosos y bienauenturados. (*Política* 56–57)

The healing touch of the Christ king has been a staple reference in the history of monarchical worship. The ceremony of the royal touch, in which kings regularly laid their hands on the sick to relieve them of their illness, had, from medieval times, been common practice in England and France (Bloch). This custom was not followed in Spain because of its incompatibility with Catholic doctrine. Yet Quevedo subverts the limitations placed on the absolutist monarch by Counter-Reformation political theory. He exemplifies the ultimate instrumentality of mystical discourses that at once make the king's body continuous with that of Christ and establish an insurmountable distance between it and his subjects.

Rulership, then, is the art not of skillful negotiation, but of "controlling experience," to borrow from Freedberg's and Stoichita's analyses of the audience response incited by pictorial representations of mystical visions. In his every gesture and utterance, Quevedo's king impresses upon his subjects the fact that his knowledge is infinite and theirs extremely limited. Jesus's response to Peter—"No sabeis lo que pedis" (qtd. in *Política* 93)—a statement that is repeated, much like a refrain, in the course of several pages, sums up the intent of the king's language to preserve the mysteries of his divine condition. His decisions are transmitted as direct decrees from God and not as the products of human calculation. In this sense, they are not to be decoded by those around him. Whereas Quevedo's contemporaries place the king in temporal history, making him beholden to human ethical and juridical systems, Quevedo envisions him as transcending these frameworks. The political instrumentality of Christ lies not in his ethical discourse, which was recovered by the humanists, but rather in his existence as a charismatic body.

Quevedo does not propose an allegorical or analogical relationship between the king and sacred symbols of power. Instead, he posits the voice and person of the sovereign as virtual extensions of a holy source. Amply useful to my formulation of the connection between language and power is Paul de Man's definition of the symbol. In contrast with allegory, says de Man, "its structure is that of the synecdoche, for the symbol is always a part of the totality that it represents. Consequently, in the symbolic imagination, no disjunction of the constitutive faculties takes place, since the material perception and the symbolical imagination are continuous" (191). In this scheme, metaphysical truth has a palpable form. Samuel Taylor Coleridge's proposition of the Scriptures as an invaluable guide for the ruling elites further serves as an illustrative point of comparison. Faith, we surmise from the following passage, is elicited by the illusion of a "being" that precedes reason. Because it leads the audience to commune with such a being that simultaneously constitutes and transcends law, the language of Holy Writ is championed by Coleridge as an antidote to utilitarianism. The "particular rules and prescripts set down in the Old Testament," he proclaims in *The Statesman's Manual,*

> flow directly and visibly from universal principles, as from a fountain: they flow from principles and ideas that are not so properly said to be confirmed by reason as to be reason itself! [. . .] Secondly, from the very nature of these principles, as taught in the Bible, they are understood in exact proportion as they are believed and felt. The regulator is never separated from the main spring. For the words of the apostle are literally and philosophically true: WE (that is, the human race) LIVE BY FAITH. Whatever we do or know, that in kind is different from the brute creation, has its origin in a determination of the reason to have

faith and trust in itself. This, its first act of faith is scarcely less than identical with its own being. [. . .] It is itself, therefore, the realizing principle, the spiritual substratum of the whole complex body of truths. This primal act of faith is enunciated in the word, GOD: a faith not derived from experience, but its ground and source. (17–18)

In sum, the power of religious rhetoric and hence its political instrumentality reside in its capacity to enact an ontological connection to a vital origin. If the hermeneutical task of the Church fathers continues to be of such use to the Counter-Reformation rhetoricians, it is because it serves as a model for the preservation of a mystical entity. Utterly moved, the audience becomes part of the communicative event, as opposed to judging its merits from a distance. In other words, we have here a version of Gadamer's notion that language "speaks through us," rather than we through language (474–75), insofar as the preacher captivates his audience by acting as a medium for spontaneously imparting the divine word that passes through him, instead of giving the impression of strategically fabricating seductive speech. The point of Gadamer's assertion is to show that there is no prelinguistic or extralinguistic knowledge, that because knowledge is generated through acquired language, it cannot be reduced to abstract concepts untouched by cultural influences (474). Where Christian oratory is concerned, the point is clearly not to present a philosophical response to scientific absolutism, but to proactively ratify the spectators' inscription within a cultural program by provoking a heightened sensation of a seamless experiential plenitude.

Similarly, in Quevedo's mind, the king's mission is not to clarify the letter of the law to his subjects, but rather to make them sensitive to the source of its authority. His role, in other words, is not to explain but to illustrate, not to justify but to embody. The substance of the king's authority is, in this sense, untranslatable, like the symbol: "If allegory can be defined as the representation of an expressible something by another expressible something," Gershom Scholem tells us, "the mystical symbol is an expressible representation of something that lies beyond the sphere of expression and communication, something that comes from a sphere whose face is, as it were, turned inward and away from us. A hidden and inexpressible reality finds its expression in the symbol" (27). In the universe of Quevedo's treatise, good politics would consist of deploying an ungraspable presence. In contrast with Gracián's understanding of beauty as that which delights through eluding the constraints of monolithic truth, the mysteries ciphered in Quevedo's brand of political *ingenio,* far from delighting, impress upon the spectator a terrifying distance between him and the source of authority. Ultimately, then, in the political realm, art becomes a mechanism of constraint, whose effectiveness depends on communicating a force that appears inevitable. Hence, Quevedo also differs from other mirror-of-princes writers in the extreme extent to which he fuses art and life.

Santa María spends the second chapter of *Repvblica y policia christiana* driving home the point that the authority of the king is purely fictitious if he does not possess the necessary qualities for good leadership: "Vn Rey vestido de purpura con grande magestad sentado en vn trono, conforme a su grādeza, graue, seuero, y terrible en la aparencia, y en el hecho todo nada. Como pintura de mano del Griego, que puesta en alto, y mirada de lexos, parece muy bien, y representa mucho; pero de cerca todo es rayas y borrones" (15). In a similar vein, Saavedra Fajardo recounts, "Tan terrible se mostró en una audiencia el rey Asuero a la reina Ester, que cayó desmayada. Y fue menester, para que volviese en sí, que, reducido por Dios a mansedumbre su espíritu descompuesto le hiciese tocar el ceptro, para que viese que no era más que un leño dorado, y él hombre, y no visión, como había imaginado" (*Empresas* 497). But in *Política de Dios,* the distinction between the man and the vision is eliminated, for the king must ensure that his body is as much an object of veneration as that of the Messiah: "Ya le vieron debaxo del dosel en el Tabor los tres Dicipulos. Magnífico y misterioso se mostrò en Canà. Marauilloso en casa de Marta, resucitando vna vez vn alma, otra vn cuerpo" (48). Such mythical aggrandizements are the condition of his rule.

Deviating starkly from Santa María's and Saavedra Fajardo's stress on the mortal body of the king, the ultimate sign of his equality to his subjects, Quevedo is interested exclusively in preserving the king's visionary stature. The distance between the sovereign and his subjects must never be diminished. Their bodies are under no circumstances exchangeable, as is implied in Quevedo's quotation from the Gospel of John, "Ni para los pobres se ha de quitar del Rey" (qtd. in *Política* 59), an adage that is vividly exemplified in Mary's adoration of Christ, a scene drawn from the same text. "Maria tomò vna libra de vnguento precioso de confeccion de Nardo, y vngio a Iesus los pies, y los limpiò con sus cabellos, y llenose la casa de fragancia con el vnguento" (qtd. in Quevedo, *Política* 59). Once again, Quevedo contravenes the modesty mandated by Spanish royal protocol under which the king was neither anointed nor idolized. The transgression becomes all the more glaring in light of Mary's unrestrained and self-effacing bodily worship, which clashes with the decorum maintained at the Habsburg court, where physical contact with the king was strictly minimized, to the extent that even his clothing was kept hidden from view and washed in isolation "de modo que el agua del río no haya tocado antes otra ropa" (Redondo 114). Yet the idolatrous homage depicted by Quevedo, at the same time, endorses the powers of corporeal self-possession, for it is through an extreme sublimation of the passions that the king kindles such ardent devotion. It is through transcending the impulses of the mortal body that he succeeds in becoming a living incarnation of the allegories of cosmic power depicted in triumphal emblems and paintings. At once unreachable and invasive, his presence conquers his flock mentally and physically.

THE POWER OF THE PASSION

> Therefore, my beloved, just as you have always obeyed me, not only in my presence, but much more now in my absence, work out your own salvation with fear and trembling.
> —Philippians 2:12

IN PART II OF QUEVEDO'S *POLÍTICA DE DIOS*, the image of the tormented martyr emerges as foremost symbol of supreme rulership: "'De la casa deste perverso le llevaron atado a la de Caifas, donde el Principe de los Sacerdotes, y todo el Concilio solicitavan hallar vn falso testimonio contra Iesus, para entregarle a la muerte.' [. . .] Hizieron burla del, taparonle los ojos, escupieronle, davanle bofetadas en la cara, y dezianle, adivinasse quien le dava" (168). Diverging from the political imaginary of the first part, here Quevedo's king abandons courtly decorum, significantly changing the face of royalty. Whereas, in part I, the Rex Sacerdos has the qualities of a wily power broker, whose prudent words and restrained gestures keep his enemies at bay and ensure the unconditional reverence of his followers, in part II, royal charisma is modeled in the image of the humiliated Christ, betrayed by his followers and persecuted by the authorities.[1] Discretion is displaced by humility, patience, and compassion. The king is urged to bear his cross and forgive his enemies. Part II ends, quite significantly, with a story about the kindness of Alfonso the Wise toward the citizens of Gaeta. Going against the recommendations of his advisers to continue the siege on this city that was key to the conquest of Naples, the king demands that hostilities be stopped and that the citizens receive good treatment from the soldiers: "No vine a pelear contra niños, mugeres, viejos, ni enfermos: por esse camino no solo quiero perder a Gaeta, y al Reyno de Napoles, mas dexara la conquista del mundo" (Quevedo, *Política* 314).

How should we interpret this shift? Is Quevedo renouncing the possibility of a Spanish "imperio universale" (Campanella 24)? Far from it. As in the first part, the main concern is the construction of a sensorially compelling monarchical authority, capable of securing public loyalty. Ever attentive to political juncture, Quevedo creates a myth of devout rulership that maintains the universal and teleological stature of monarchy while responding quite specifically to the growing despondence that accompanies the middle and later years of Olivares's regime. Quevedo finds a suitable symbol in the meek figure of the Ecce Homo and the wounded body of the Crucifixion. The physical and mental scenarios he evokes in this part of the work are strongly grounded in public and private devotional practices that focus on the agony of Christ. Like these practices, as well as the spiritual breviaries, processional sculptures, and visionary paintings related to them, Quevedo's text promotes a passionate exchange between sacred being and worshiper. Its particular fusion of theology and politics, moreover, differs significantly from the brand of *pietas* displayed in royal iconographic programs as well as from the king's own religious practices.

Written between 1635 and 1639, more than a decade after part I of *Politica de Dios,* part II relates to a somewhat different set of historical and biographical circumstances. The first part, we will remember, can be linked to a moment of transition between the governments of Philip III and Philip IV when there is hope that the new king will do away with the ills of the previous regime. But by the mid-1630s, such optimism has worn thin, with Olivares's failures. The costs of his aggressive military policies have drained state coffers and alienated the nobles, who are forced to bear the added financial burden (Elliott, *The Count-Duke* 590–93). Quevedo's rejection of realpolitik is also informed by the fact that he has now fallen out of favor with the court; yet this does not invalidate the text's larger significance as an epochal reflection on the changing meaning of political ritual.

By the middle years of Olivares's term, the notion that the king has limited agency is yet more acutely felt than in previous years. In addition to the ongoing cultural trends mentioned in the previous chapter—the growing use of paper and print, the rise of the bureaucrat, the increasingly impersonal face of government, the withdrawal of the king—the sheer accumulation of political and economic setbacks has made the gap between symbolic power and effective power all the more glaring. Moreover, the count-duke's unpopular revenue policies—privileging the sanctity of the state over that of prominent individuals—has by this time embittered much of the ruling elite. The *donativos* mandated in 1632 and 1635 severely affected the running of the Casa Real (Stradling 138–39): the withholding of wages from a number of royal officials and servants bred discontent and scandal. Despite

Olivares's attempts to redress the damage, the symbolic role of the court was irrevocably compromised.

In the following years, with the Portuguese and Catalonian revolts and repeated defeats in the Thirty Years' War, the authority of the king came under unprecedented attack: "The royal prestige was assailed, and even the question of Philip's rightful sovereignty *as king* was not left untouched by a mounting tide of sedition and complaint. Overt disrespect for the royal office was previously almost unknown in Spain, but that such a phenomenon should now become discernable, indeed amounting at times to contempt and open defiance, is perhaps not surprising" (Stradling 231). Among the most blatant indications of the monarch's weakened status is the attempted regicide in 1645 (Stradling 232). With this in mind, the closing episode recounted in *Política de Dios* about a king who forgives his potential assassin acquires added topical relevance.

Informed by a pronounced awareness of historical and cultural crisis, part II of *Política de Dios* seeks a form of political figuration that can conserve the illusion of a vital organic connection between the failing monarch and his people. Otherwise said, it constitutes an attempt to rescue the king's auratic function at a time when court culture is all too easily revealed to be empty artifice.

Redefining the Courtly Body

The image of Louis XIV, Peter Burke tells us, was repeatedly modified to fit distinct stages of his long reign (*The Fabrication*). During his first years, Louis is captured in pictures that emphasize his youth; as he reaches maturity, he is cast in more stately poses. Subsequently, there ensues what Burke terms a "crisis in representation" (*The Fabrication* 126), that is, a protracted debate on whether the sovereign ought to be presented as a mythical figure or be dressed in modern garb. The quarrel of the ancients and the moderns does not, of course, play out like this in Spain, in the sense that there are not two mutually opposed camps defining themselves in these terms. However, the notion of such a crisis is relevant to an analysis of the Spanish context insofar as there coexist diverse conceptions of political image construction that tend to be fraught with awareness of unsettling change. It is particularly useful where Quevedo is concerned, given his tendency to polarize cultural tensions. Promoting an image of messianic rulership far more extreme than the one associated with Olivares's previously cited campaign to "'re-Catholicize'" (Feros, "'Sacred'" 80) Habsburg rule by playing up Philip

IV's role as Defender of the Faith, Quevedo defines the Defensor Fidei in trenchant opposition to the language of courtly splendor and decorum.

For all its condemnation of court society, for all its ranting against dissembling politicians, part II of *Politica de Dios* is anything but an indictment of the theatricality of power. It alters the symbolic register of corporeal display precisely to attain a more gripping form of exhibition. It is from this perspective that we must understand its opposition of the mundane and the divine orders, an intent well noted by the writer of the prologue: "¡Grande batalla! Dios con el mundo, el espiritu con la carne, la verdad con la presuncion, la Iglesia con los Principes, y Señores del mundo" (qtd. in Quevedo, *Política* 139).

Amplifying a topic already latent in part I, part II forges a dichotomy between the figure of the ideal king, who is identified with an apostolic mission, and the evil ministers, who are associated to courtly protocol and reason of state, which are, in turn, explicitly identified with the legacy of "Iudios, Escrivas, y Fariseos" (Quevedo, *Política* 168). Far from the glorious sanctum of the planet king, his palaces are compared to tombs and to the gallows: "Los Palacios para el Principe ocioso, son sepulcros de vna vida muerta, y para el que atiende son patibulo de vna muerte viva" (Quevedo, *Política* 211). The counselors who keep the unwary king shielded from the problems of state and from the larger public are maligned as the greatest of all evils. "¿Quantos leprosos de conciencia quieren cerrar a todo el Rey en su casa: y para que no le participen los que le buscan, y tienen necessidad del, los calumnian, y acusan, y desacreditan?" (Quevedo, *Política* 157). It is they who are ultimately responsible for the corruption of the political arena. The monarch is thereby urged to break with the courtly stage and connect with a larger public, assuming his God-given role as "padre de los huerfanos, y de las viudas, que son mudos" (Quevedo, *Política* 165).

Such conceits would contrast starkly with the traditional syncretic imagery associated with the Sun King and his dynasty. The pervasiveness of Greco-Roman allegorical tropes in Habsburg propaganda is well represented in a description of the Huesca festivities held in honor of Prince Felipe Próspero's birth. Events featured included both religious processions in which effigies of saints were carried and classical pageantry. Moreover, Catholicism and pagan antiquity were intermingled in much of the scenery. Particularly illustrative of this is the account of one of the allegories of Spain, represented by "vna Matrona robusta, armada con vn morrion dorado," at whose feet the symbols of the different provinces, themselves assembled along a zodiacal wheel, would fall when they were at their highest elevation (*Relacion de las fiestas* 12):

> Estaba España en rico, i Magestoso trono, cuyo dosel era de lama verde, i oro bordado con admirable destreça, la frente del dosel tenia bordadas diferentes empressas del amor, i la gotera variedad de frutas, i flores i vnos Cupidos, que a manos llenas las arrojavan sobre España. [. . .] A los pies del trono de España bajo de la rueda de la fortuna estava esta inscripcion.
> *Rinda todo el Orbe el clavo*
> *su cerviz a mi fortuna,*
> *pues a su rueda importuna*
> *le puso un Principe el clavo.*
> [. . .] A mano derecha se descubria la celebrada Huesca, Oscense, que es lo mismo que dezir el Parnaso de dos puntas, a cuyo pie se levantava un laurel frondoso de sesenta palmos de alto, a su sombra estava Apolo, tocando su Lira, coronado del dorado desden de su ingrata Dafne, rodeado de las nueve Musas, representadas por hermosas Doncellas, vestidas de telas ricas, con coronas de laurel. (*Relacion de las fiestas* 12–13)

Through the symbols of agricultural prosperity and artistic plenitude deriving from stock Roman representations of political rebirth and imperial apogee, Spanish might is associated with material and secular preeminence. From such celebratory pomp, part II of *Política de Dios* diverges acutely, designing a political theater that is Christocentric in a sense yet more absolute than in part I. Although it is true that in that initial text Quevedo claims to adhere solely to "las acciones y palabras de Christo" (40), he endows Christ with the corporeal magnificence of the Sun King. Rejecting such visions of triumphalism, part II confronts us with a pitiful lacerated royal body. It promotes a militant asceticism that can, among other things, be understood as a critique of the considerable expenditure and effort devoted by Olivares to the construction of a new royal palace, the Buen Retiro.

In February 1637, in an attempt to weather political crisis through ostentation, the Buen Retiro was finally inaugurated with sumptuous festivities that opened with the torchlight parade of the king and two hundred nobles. In the masquerade that followed at the new arena of the Prado Alto, manifestations of royal splendor abounded. "The arena, illuminated by over six thousand torches and glazed lanterns, was surrounded by a two-tiered wooden structure divided into 488 loggias. The woodwork was painted to make it look like silver, bronze, jasper and marble, and the arena was decorated with emblematic devices. [Bernardo] Monanni picked out the king's device of the sun, with its inscription 'I warm and shine' [. . .] and the count-duke's of the sunflower, inclining toward the sun" (Brown and Elliott 200). Equally grand were the celebrations held on several subsequent days, which included plays, poetry competitions, pageants, dances, and bullfights.

Where the festivities surrounding the inauguration culminate in carnival celebrations (Brown and Elliott 200), Quevedo chooses another, more somber, more purely Christian moment of the calendar as the most adequate referent for communal healing: "S. Marcos dize: 'Salvum fac temetipsum descendens de Cruce. Salvate a ti mismo descendiendo de la Cruz.' Assi dizen todos los malos que assisten al lado de los Reyes: 'Salvate à ti, y a nosotros con baxarte, Señor.' Vasallo que pide a su Rey que se baxe, alçarse quiere. El baxarse de la Cruz el Principe, es quitarse, y derribarse de la tarea, y fatiga de su oficio" (*Política* 221).

We will remember that the main scenes of part I—the wedding at Cana, the touching of Jesus's robe, the Messiah's anointment, the humiliation of Jacob and John—portray a Messiah who conforms to the codes of royal composure, one who assumes a commanding and distant guise that is perfectly in line with the strict verbal and corporeal self-control required of the successful courtier. Like part I, part II is emphatically body centered, but this time Quevedo's "countertextual" (Berger 163) poetics, with their insistence on physical and psychological pain, are charged with a violence emblematic of the clash between temporality and transcendence. Ultimately, that violence becomes the condition of their transcendence.

From History to Eschatology

Jean-Marie Apostolidès has read the artifice of the French court as an effort to shut out mortality, to safeguard the symbolic sphere of the palace from the instabilities of the historical process. Referring to the physical appearance of the courtier, he comments,

> Son corps est transformé par les vêtements de cour, qui sont des excroissances des formes naturelles. Le courtisan se définit au premier regard par la capacité physique d'exhiber un surplus. Ainsi, la longue

perruque bouclée est-elle une exagération du système capillaire normal; les paniers des robes forment une excroissance des hanches féminines, les talons hauts augmentent la taille. La multiplicité des jupons, semblables à des rideaux de scène, souligne l'aspect théâtral de la stature. [. . .] Le courtisan se construit comme un château, tout en façade; il ne donne son plein effet que regardé à une certaine distance. [. . .] Le courtisan est une essence qui échappe à la dégradation historique. (*Le roi-machine* 52–53)

Even though some features of French court fashions and rituals are not present in Spain, the gist of Apostolidès's argument holds true there as well. The links between artifice, good taste, and everlasting world dominion are well entrenched in Madrid, which considers itself a foremost center of world patronage. In *Sólo Madrid es corte,* don Alonso Núñez de Castro sings the praises of his court as a capital of the exquisite:

Fabrique en buen hora Londres los paños de mas estimacion, Olanda los Cábrais, sus raxas Florencia, la India los castores y vicuñas, Milan los brocados, Italia, y Flandes las estatuas, y los lienços, que ponen à pleyto à los originales la vida, como lo goze nuestra Corte; que solo pruevan con esso, que todas las Naciones crían oficiales para Madrid, y que es señora de las Cortes. [. . .]

Enriquece à las forasteras Naciones con su plata, y oro, porque ellas la sirvan al gusto en la invencion de los manjares, y bebidas, al olfato en las fragrácias, à los ojos en los milagros del pincel, y de la escultura, al oido con los mas celebrados Musicos del Orbe, à la ostétacion con las telas, y piedras preciosas; pero essos gastos no la malquistan de prodiga en el sentir acertado de Aristoteles, sino de discreta en conocer à que fin se destinò el oro, y el uso legitimo de las riquezas. (15)

In Quevedo's definition of political legitimacy, divergently, true magnificence is explicitly divorced from material splendor: "Muchos entienden que reynan, porque se ven con cetro, corona, y purpura (insignias de la Magestad, y superficie delgada de aquel oficio) y siendo verdugos de sus Imperios, y provincias, los dexa Dios el nombre, y las ceremonias, para que conozcan las gentes, que pidieron estas insignias para adorno de su calamidad, y de su ruina" (*Política* 153–54). The court is no longer detached from temporal ruin.

The apocalyptic strain of part I, it is important to note, does continue in part II, as in the following passage, where the king is presented as ushering his kingdom into an age of redemption:

> Preguntaron a Iesus, "¿Si era el prometido, el que avia de venir?" Y Cristo respondiò con obras sin palabras. Pues luego resuscitò muertos, dio vista a ciegos, pies a tullidos, habla a los mudos, salud a los enfermos, libertad a los posseidos del Demonio. Y después dixo: "Id, y direis a Iuan, que los muertos resucitan, los ciegos ven, los mudos hablan, los tullidos andan, los enfermos guarecen." Quien a todos dà, y a nadie quita: quien a todos dà lo que les falta [. . .] esse Rey es, esse es el Prometido: es el que se espera, y con el no ay mas que esperar. Pobladas estan de coronas, y cetros estas acciones. (Quevedo, *Política* 164)

No contemporary could fail to recognize the allusion to the rampant problems of economic distribution that were the bane of Philip IV's reign. In this rhetorical tour de force that fuses together particular temporal circumstances and eschatological paradigms, the solution to these problems—that is, giving to all what they need and not taking from anyone—is equated with fulfillment of the sacred prophecy. Time comes to a stop: "No hay más que esperar." Several references to Jesus's portentous and humble birth and his assimilation to the sun or a rising star also serve to recall the king's embodiment of a new era of plenitude. "Que es vn Rey, vna estrella del cielo, que alumbra la tierra, norte de los subditos, con cuya luz, è influencia viven; por esso apareciò estrella a los tres Reyes. Todos los Reyes (Señor) son Estrellas del Sol Cristo Iesus; familia suya son resplandeciente" (Quevedo, *Política* 214).

On a certain level, such apotheotic imagery can be read as an appropriation of Habsburg panegyrical iconography that brought the symbology of cosmic power together with that of Christian devotion. A particularly famous example of this would be El Greco's *Dream of Philip II,* which was painted in commemoration of the 1571 victory at Lepanto (fig. 6). In the center foreground, a kneeling Philip II looks up at the heavens, where a multitude of saints and martyrs are assembled. The king's gaze converges with that of the celestial company in adoration of the shining cross that sits upon the Habsburg "IHS." The earthly victory over the Turks, whose dead bodies are piled up behind and below Philip II, is thus directly linked to a cosmic triumph of Christianity over infidelity (Tanner 204). In a similar vein, Jeronimus Wierix's engraving of Philip II kneeling beside Pope Gregory XIII as they receive a globe from Christ directly aligns

FIG 6. El Greco, *The Dream of Philip II*, 1579. Monasterio de San Lorenzo, Escorial, Madrid. Photo: Erich Lessing / Art Resource, New York.

Habsburg dynasty with ecclesiastical power, global domination, and messianic mission (fig. 7).

On the other hand, Quevedo's pious king and the royal figures represented in encomiastic art diverge in important ways. We note that in El Greco's apotheotic vision as in Wierix's, the king is shown as a composed

FIG 7. Jeronimus Wierix, *Christ Gives the Symbols of Power to Philip II in the Presence of Pope Gregory XIII*, 1667. Bibliothèque royale de Belgique.

figure. By contrast, Quevedo's king is fashioned in the image of Christ as a pathos-ridden scapegoat. In a manner analogous to the blinded Oedipus or the imprisoned Antigone, the tormented Christ king embodies the pangs of the historical process. As Apostolidès so aptly puts it in his analysis of the relationship between classical theater and the political framework of absolutist France, "Nous apercevons déjà comment l'image du roi devient le lieu imaginaire, à la charnière du physique et du psychique, du collectif et de l'individuel, qui permet d'unir ce que la pratique politique de l'Etat naissant dissocie. Elle seule en effet assure la réconciliation du *rex* et du *sacerdos*" (*Le prince* 25). Referring to the tragedies of Racine as a reflection on the emergence of the modern state, Apostolidès notes the parallels between the conflict of a heroic legendary past with a historical present, dramatized in the bloody anagnorisis of the tragic hero of antiquity and the preoccupations of the seventeenth-century political elite caught between medieval chivalric ideals and the requirements of a new institutional order. These tensions are clearly at issue in part II, where the figure of the martyred Christ can be interpreted as a form of resistance to some of the dominant social and cultural practices implicated in the development of the state. At issue is not only the dissociation between the secular and sacred orders that occurs with administrative and bureaucratic expansion, but also its repercussions within the realm of the "lieu imaginaire." Vis-à-vis the inability of palatine art and ceremony to guarantee the authority of the king, Quevedo suggests a change of register: he envisions a king who cleanses the body politic by atoning for its sins with his own mind and body: "O si tuvieran voz los arrepentimientos de los Monarcas, que yazen mudos en el silencio de la muerte; ¿quantos gritos se oyeran de sus conciencias?" (*Política* 177).

Visible here is a turn away from the stoic bent of part I, as the heightened expression of pain that decorum would want repressed is brought to light. Discovering in Shakespeare's *King Lear* a sustained justification of affect, Richard Strier holds that, far from being maligned as a sign of weakness, emotional outpour is prevalent among the virtuous characters; it is the villains who practice discretion, strategically holding back their true sentiments (36). Similarly, in part II of *Política de Dios,* Quevedo portrays the evil ministers who betray the king as representatives of a deviant *razón de estado,* crafty dissimulators who attempt to confine the sovereign to his palace, hidden from his people, whose opinion they manipulate (157). Not unlike what occurs in *King Lear,* Quevedo's monarch suffers at the hands of his coldhearted ministers: prudence has been reduced to soulless cunning. Equal in its sensationalism to Shakespeare's overpowering dramatic rendition of a malevolent Edmund is Quevedo's declamation against scheming counselors: "*O Señor,* quan frequentemente los ministros [. . .] por satisfacer su odio en el valeroso, en el docto, en el justo, mezclan en su calumnia el nombre de Cesar, el del Rey: fingen traicion, publican rebeldia, y enojo del Principe, donde no ay vno, ni otro, para que el Cesar, y el Rey sea causa de la crueldad que no manda, de la maldad que no comete" (*Política* 173).

Quevedo's insistence on the king's victimization operates under the premise—well established by all manner of political thinkers from Machiavelli to Rivadeneira—that an emotional connection between the ruler and his subjects is central to the preservation of his reign. Considering epochal ideas on the usefulness of artistic imitation to this goal, Victoria Kahn shows how Guarini's aesthetic theory "suggests that artistic representation contains a key to negotiating the imperfect world of human passions and interests" (224). Indeed, the creative portrayal of the king as a casualty of courtly intrigue effectively impresses his innocence upon the public mind. At the same time, much more than simply clearing him of blame, the guise of messianic humility that Quevedo urges him to don ensures his sacralization.

The Imitatio Christi as Virtual Reinactment

Toda la vida del christiano; si bive como lo manda el euangelio: cruz ha de ser y penitencia.

—Domingo de Valtanás, *Confessionario*

As we read Quevedo's passages about how the king must bear his cross and inspire his ministers to suffer as he does, it is well to remember the ubiquitous presence of Cross worship in the early modern world and its deep conditioning of the Spanish social fabric. The prevalence of Passion and Crucifixion scenes in sixteenth- and seventeenth-century painting and drama can be taken as a reflection of their central importance in people's intimate lives. From the countless devotional guides and rituals through which Christian doctrine was spread and materialized, we can surmise that Christ's martyrdom is among the main organizing principles of both private and public life. It is, moreover, a symbol that cuts across class lines, connecting to a cultural universe that exists beyond the court.

As is evident from the history of Counter-Reformation Christianity, the imitation of Christ is by no means reserved exclusively for the king. From the founding of the desert monastic communities of late antiquity, the reliving of Christ's torment as a means to reach God would become a seminal component of religious identity. The routine mortification of the flesh, the voluntary abstention from nourishment, and the forfeiting of social success are among the ways in which early Christians break with the accepted avenues of prestige of the classical world. We have only to think of the emaciated Saint Anthony, submitting himself to physical pain, hunger, and solitude, or the martyred Saint Felicitas, relishing in the tortures of the gladiatorial combat, to visualize the way in which Christianity conceives of itself as a rejection of established forms of knowledge and authority. The divide between heaven and earth is redrawn, Peter Brown tells us, as the "'upperworldly'" is defined in opposition to the worldly (2). Saint Anthony, for instance, rails against learned culture, opposing it to faith, considered the only vehicle for divine inspiration (Athanasius the Great 101–4). Even Saint Augustine, who paradoxically devotes much of his career to welding together classical and Christian institutional structures, understands Christian revelation as turning away from influential public rhetoric to internal meditation (*Confessions* 39; 52).

Of course, this is just one of the faces of Catholicism. If Christianity is in its beginnings a stateless religion, it capitalizes on the cultural practices of the classical world as it becomes institutionalized, which can be clearly seen in the syncretic iconographies of the Catholic state. But, in some terrains, the eschatological radicalism of early Christianity prevails, ever rigidly emphasizing the line between heaven and earth. In certain religious processions, as in private rituals of penance, the infliction of bodily and psychological pain plays a crucial role. In medieval and early modern Europe, the Crucifixion becomes an object of worship and imitation in its own right. As Susan Verdi Webster notes, in Spanish Corpus Christi and Easter celebrations, images of the crucified Christ would be paraded through the streets accompanied by processants who would act out the plight of the Messiah in a variety of ways. Early on, they would reenact the Passion by carrying the Cross. Later, as the confraternities participating in the processions grew, they would represent specific moments of the Crucifixion (Webster 95). A common feature of the processions were the groups of flagellants, who would lash their exposed backs with wood and leather sticks. The images and sculptures made for these occasions also tell a revealing story about the extent to which the imitatio Christi is conceived as a material performance. Working under the demand that their artwork must have "'la apariencia de ser vivo'" (Webster 108), the creators of processional sculptures fabricate pieces that give the illusion of physical precision. Often, the sculptures would have contraptions that allowed for mimicking of the actual poses of Christ. For instance, the Christ figure produced by a certain Agustín Muñoz for Good Friday processions is especially equipped to enact the descent from the Cross. His patron, the Santo Entierro Confraternity, made precise stipulations about how the hands must fall to the sides when unnailed and how the shoulders must not appear marked (Webster 67). In short, as Webster points out, based on contracts and instructions to sculptors, the realism with which the act of humility is represented is perceived to have a direct impact on its ability to induce faith in the audience.

Distinctions between Christ and the re-creation of Christ are erased, insofar as contact with the icon is made equivalent to communion with divine being itself (Freedberg; Gallego; Bertelli). The same assumption applies in secular pictorial theory, as reflected in Giulio Mancini's *Considerazioni sulla pittura,* which, David Freedberg tells us, contends that erotic pictures "well-made and of the right temper" should be placed in the bedroom because they would stimulate man and woman to have "beautiful, healthy, and charming children" (3). Mancini's conception of artistic imitation approaches Gadamer's eucharistic definition of being, which incorporates art as a vital force, regards not as "a copy so much as the appearance of what is presented. [. . .] In presentation, the presence of what is presented reaches its consummation" (137). Invalidating the possibility of abstract truths that exist a priori, beyond the realm of cultural practice, Gadamer, as previously pointed out, situates truth in this realm. To the Kantian notion of mimesis as the translation of an idea, he thereby opposes a view of artistic imitation as the living essence of an idea that exists in dynamic form, through contact with its audience. In its emphasis on the interactive dimension of art and in its endowment of the particular and subjective instance of artistic reception with supreme conceptual and existential density, Gadamer's definition of art—notwithstanding its stress on interpretive flexibility—bears comparison with David Kertzer's definition of ritual: "Through ritualized action, the inner becomes outer, and the subjective world picture becomes a social reality" (9). In both cases, sensorial representation has the stature of irrefutable being.

Catholic rhetoricians would understand the power of words similarly, convinced as they were that masterful oratory could have transformative effects on their audience. As Juan de Borja held in his *Empresas morales,* "Mucho mayor fuerça tienen, para persuadir, los exemplos, que las palabras, y los hombres se persuaden, y dexan llevar mas, de lo que veen, que de lo que oyen" (322). More than an attack on verbal communication in itself, this assertion is best understood as a reflection on the importance of sensorial illusion, something that can, in addition, be achieved through words. Indeed, also clear from this affirmation is the extent to which the precepts formulated in rhetorical and pictorial manuals converge with those preached in moral or spiritual advice books.

As widely recognized, it is through fixing specific images and situations in their minds, rather than through debating abstract ideas, that people are driven to certain attitudes and actions. Many of the spiritual breviaries, which are the bestsellers of the time, recommend that the faithful should form a mental picture of Christ's suffering and subsequently surrender to the sentiments that it elicits in them. From Thomas à Kempis's *Imitatio Christi* to Juan de Ávila's *Lecciones,* Fray Domingo de Valtanás's *Confessionario,* and Saint Ignatius's *Ejercicios espirituales,* to name but a few examples, emphasis falls on spirituality as an interiorized and exteriorized experience. Discussing private meditational programs, Freedberg says that "they were substantially practical, since readers and adherents were consistently instructed to transform simple meditation into commitment to the *imitatio Christi.* Christ was a doer, not simply a preacher of abstract parables: even the parables themselves brought abstraction to earth. [. . .] From now on, even when not specifically stated, even before its massive reinvigoration in the work of Ignatius of Loyola, imitation becomes a central recommendation in almost all the treatises and handbooks" (174). Accordingly, the function of art is seen as a fundamental component of spiritual education, for it moves the worshiper to imitate Christ (see Mujica Pinilla). The highly emotional relationship of early Christians to their religious icons, explains Peter Brown, replicates in a divine terrain the close ties of *amicitia* on which personal patronage was built. Specifically, the foundation of the Christian community is predicated in terms of the gratuitous bonds of filial love, an intimate communion between the self and divinity. Hence the pervasiveness of practices that center on a personal contact with the pain and suffering of Jesus and the martyred saints. The following account of a late antique Carthaginian pilgrim at Saint Stephen's shrine stands as an eloquent example of how the ongoing reassertion of sacrality is materialized in modes of worship: "While she prayed at the place of the holy relic shrine, she beat against it, not only with the longings of her heart, but with her whole body so that the little grille in front of the relic opened at the impact; and she, taking the Kingdom of Heaven by storm, pushed her head inside and laid it on the holy relics resting there, drenching them with her tears" (qtd. in P. Brown 88).

Likewise, in Quevedo's universe, the king must by no means settle for being a diminished copy of divinity. The ideal king must be the very opposite of "el Pastor que ni vè, ni guia, ni toca a sus ovejas" (*Política* 201). He is the antithesis of the lifeless idols decried in the Psalms: "The idols of the nations are silver and gold, / the work of human hands. / They have mouths, but they do not speak; / they have eyes, but they do not see; / they have ears, but they do not hear, / and there is no breath in their mouths. / Those who make them and all who trust them shall become like them" (135:15–18). Quevedo's king evinces sacrality, rendering it an immediate reality before his audience. He becomes his real self, assumes his true being as the sacramental body of Christ, through contemplating images of the Messiah, just as his subjects attain sanctity as inhabitants of the New Jerusalem by communing with his example. In Quevedo's own words, "Lo que se manda se oye, lo que se vè, se imita" (*Política* 283). Here "word and image are not mere imitative illustrations, but allow what they present to be for the first time fully what it is" (Gadamer 143). Audience and object intermingle, attaining wholeness in one another. This intermingling, in turn, acquires a more pronounced physicality and emotionality in comparison with part I of the treatise. If there the king, although a pervasive physical presence, was ultimately beyond reach, here he openly invites intense somatic contact.

FIG 8. Caravaggio, *Doubting Thomas*, 1601–2. Stiftung Preussische Schlösser, Brandenburg. Photo: Bildarchiv Preussicher Kulturbesitz / Art Resource, New York.

Symptomatic of this turn would be the contrast between the scene in part I where the humble woman gently touches the robe of the imperious Messiah, and the scene in part II where the wayward apostle dips his hands into Christ's wounds. In the first case, the woman touches his garments of her own initiative; in the second, Christ expressly asks his disciple to lay his hands on him. The difference between the kinds of touch depicted in the two scenes is also of obvious import; Quevedo makes the invasiveness of Thomas's handling quite plain: "Empero dudar Tomas Apostol que huviesse resucitado, y dezir, que si no vè las señales de los clavos, y entra la mano en su costado, que no lo ha de creer: y mandarle Cristo N. S. resucitado, glorioso, impassible, que metiesse la mano en su costado, y manosease sus llagas, es hazaña de la paciencia Divina, que excede toda ponderacion, adonde se desalienta el espanto" (*Política* 259). The use of the verb "manosear" leaves us no room to doubt the intended emphasis on the infringement of the body. Like Caravaggio's famous rendering of the scene (fig. 8), Quevedo's narrative foregrounds the violated anatomy of the king.[2]

Glenn Most points out that in the Gospel of John there is no evidence that Thomas actually touched Christ (57). The Messiah invites him to touch his body, but the Gospel does not state that Thomas proceeds to do so. It is centuries of theological exegesis and pictorial representations that establish that Thomas literally laid his hands on the Messiah. These interpretations tell us much more about late antique, medieval, and Counter-Reformation Christianity than they do about the Gospel of John: they attest to the paradoxical importance of physicality in a religious tradition that condemns the material realm.

For Quevedo, the paradoxical role of tactile experience is of infinite value in the political realm. Indeed, he singles out the Doubting Thomas episode as his treatise's most important lesson: "Por ser este capitulo el mas importante desta Politica para todos, y particularmente para los Reyes, y Monarcas, busquè con atenta consideracion en toda la vida de Cristo Nuestro Señor, que toda fue paciencia desde el nacer al morir, lugar en que autorizar mi discurso: y por el mas encarecido de su soberana, inmensa, y benigna paciencia, escogi este del Apostol Santo Tomas" (*Política* 258). To the claim that the episode is of such value because it exemplifies infinite patience, we might add that its primordial interest, to a great extent, lies in its representation of a form of corporeal presence that overcomes the limitations of royal aloofness by arriving at a formulation of the monarchical body that, more current with adverse times, preserves its humanness. Supremely polysemic—interpretable at once as the ultimate humiliation of the Messiah and as superlative proof of his authority—Thomas's act rises to the challenges of myth making in a waning regime. Exploiting the capacious referentiality of carnal sensation, the episode fluctuates between connotations of the profane, symbolized in Thomas's need for material proof of divinity and in the portrayal of Christ's lacerated body as continuous with that of the mortal sinner, and of the sacred, ciphered in the Messiah's oozing wounds taken as undeniable demonstrations of his mystical resurrection. Focusing on the history of touch in the early modern period, Elizabeth Harvey stresses its fluidity, its reflection of "the dialectic between materiality and resurrection" (1). On the one hand, "the sense most resolutely yoked to corporeality or materiality" (Harvey 21), touch is repressed or at least strictly regimented during the rise of the modern state in a social process that hinges upon a rationalized control of instinctual biological impulses. The conventions of composure and decorous aloofness that were the hallmark of courtly conduct signify the sublimation of human contact. And yet sentient corporeality continues to have an extraordinarily important role in the construction authority: "Touch, perhaps more than any other sense, is a mediator—between the body and what transcends it" (Harvey 21).

Otherwise said, the physical body as palpable organism is perceived as a privileged incarnation of mental aspirations.

In sum, the "civilizing process" constitutes only one mode of sanctifying the human. Quevedo, no doubt, knew that the representations of royalty emerging from court culture—the decorously sober king, the triumphal solar allegories—were no longer effective figurations of authority. In their hieratic poise or in their iconic abstraction, they could appear too removed from a suffering people to excite the right level of feeling. As shown by Juan Martínez Montañés's famous processional sculpture of the Jesús de la Pasión (fig. 9), the agonizing human body can be a far more gripping spectacle. This image of Christ, his face bleeding beneath the crown of thorns, his head bowed with emotional and physical suffering, is eminently illustrative of the kind of supreme *humilitas* that Quevedo urges his king to espouse. Human imperfection is at once recognized, materialized, and turned into a divine object of worship.

Consuming the King

In the time of the Spanish Habsburgs, the state secures its control over the feast of the Eucharist, which has become a fixed part of the Church calendar and the association between the monarchy and the worship of the Host is an ongoing motif of many an artistic program (Tanner). Symptomatic in this respect is the manner in which Pedro Calderón de la Barca's sacramental play (*auto sacramental*) *El nuevo palacio del Retiro* links the palace to the resurgence of godly grace, portraying it as center of the New Jerusalem. In the opening scene, the Man berates the Jew, emphasizing his exclusion from the nascent order:

> Ya que la fábrica altiva
> toca con el capitel
> al cielo, porque triunfante
> hoy y militante estén
> dadas de las manos, ya
> que a conseguir, ya que a ser
> llega el cumplimiento de esta
> obra el supremo pincel,
> del Viejo Palacio, que era
> sinagoga de tu Ley

FIG 9. Juan Martínez Montañés, *Jesús de la Pasión*, 1610–15. Iglesia Colegial del Divino Salvador, Seville. Photo: Alberto Fraile Carmona.

> Escrita, la Ley de Gracia
> viene llena de placer
> al Nuevo Palacio Real
> para aposentarse en él,
> adonde dicen que hoy
> con el Rey ha de comer,
> porque en un convite empiezan
> las fiestas que se han de hacer.
> Aquel cordero que tú
> comiste en Egipto en pie,
> con las lechugas amargas,
> aquí el viático es,
> comido con penitencia,
> mezclando amargura y miel,
> porque esto la letra dice
> del Fasé y Parascevé. (Calderón de la Barca, *El nuevo palacio* 111–12)

In this reference to an inaugural palatine banquet, Calderón makes full use of Christian hermeneutics, intertwining Hebrew Scripture and New Testament. The written laws of Moses are displaced by the laws of grace that lodge themselves in the royal edifice, which emerges from the blueprint of the Jewish temple. We cannot help here recalling Juan Bautista de Villalpando's influential architectural treatise *In Ezechielem explanationes, et apparatus urbis, ac templi Hierosolymitani,* whose visual and narrative re-creation of Solomon's temple posits a literal continuity between divine and human works. In an analogous fashion, the king's meal is associated by Calderón with the sacrificial lamb of Exodus, subsumed and transformed into the Holy Host. Later, the playwright further merges the figure of the king with that of the Host, drawing up a symbolic complex comprising palace, king, Eucharist, and eschatological prophecy:

> Esta blanca Forma, este
> círculo breve y pequeño,
> capaz esfera es de cuanto
> contiene hoy la tierra y cielo.
> Blanco pan fue; pero ya,
> transustanciado en mí mesmo,
> no es pan, sus especies sí,
> porque este solo es mi cuerpo. (*El nuevo palacio* 172)

Similarly, in the significance of the Host as symbol of royal sacrifice, Quevedo finds an added spectrum of metaphorical associations for his formulation of the Christ king. We should, however, distinguish Quevedo's particular exploitation of the link between king and Eucharist from that in Calderón's play, which, like El Greco's *Dream of Philip II,* stops short of actual deification of the monarch's person. The association made in the play between king and sacrament maintains its allegorical status: the king represents the sacrament without literally embodying it. After drawing the connection between the royal and the sacred bodies, the play exhibits them as two parallel and distinct entities; we note from the parenthetical stage instructions that the king stands *beside* the Host (Calderón de la Barca, *El nuevo palacio* 173). The same is true of an otherwise very different representation linking the Habsburg ruler and the sacrament, an engraving that celebrates Philip IV through a Romanized re-creation of the Corpus Christi procession, with the prince mounted on a magnificent eucharistic chariot below the monstrance, which is framed by the sun (fig. 10). Once again, the king is shown to have a privileged link with the Host, but his sacrality remains a ceremonial device.

Aiming to transcend the poetics of ceremonial convention and to empower the king with the language of active political impact, Quevedo seeks a more complete link between the historical king and the body of Christ, highlighting the significance of the Eucharist as the flesh of the Messiah: "Quien come mi carne, y bebe mi sangre, tiene vida eterna: y yo le resucitarè en el postrero dia. De verdad mi carne es comida, y de verdad mi sangre es bebida. Quien come mi carne, y bebe mi sangre, queda en mi, y yo en èl" (qtd. in *Política* 159; see also García-Bryce, *Envisioning*). Commenting on the above passage, Quevedo says, "Y si bien estas misteriosas palabras se entienden del Santissimo Sacramento de la Eucharistia: fertiles de sentidos, y de doctrina, y exemplo, me ocasionan consideracion piadosa de enseñança para todos los Principes de la tierra" (*Política* 159). Quevedo welcomes the fertility of Saint John's conceit, casting the king as a vital incarnation of the "Word made flesh." He himself remarks on the fact that his depiction of the tormented royal body might be disconcerting to some: "Estrañaràn los poderosos del mundo, que yo les represente vn Rey tendido en el potro, y dando vozes. Sea testigo el mismo Rey, oiganlo de su boca, Psalmo 37: 'Porque tus saetas en mi estàn clavadas, y descargaste sobre mi tu mano. No ay sanidad en mi carne delante de la cara de tu ira: no tienen paz mis huessos delante de la cara de mis pecados.' El mismo dize, que los cordeles se le entran por la carne, y le quiebran los huessos" (*Política* 164). Returning then to John's testimony of the coming

FIG 10. *Eucharistic Chariot*, in Lequile's *Colossvs angelicvs*, 1655. Artist unknown. Biblioteca Nacional de España.

of the Messiah, Quevedo exhorts the king to become a substantive imitation of Christ: "Verdad es, que no podeis (Señor) obrar aquellos milagros; mas tambien lo es, que podeis imitar sus efectos. Obligado estais a la imitacion de Cristo" (*Política* 165).[3] Ultimately, the difference between working miracles and imitating their effects is negligible, for Quevedo insists at length on the king's appropriation of the persona of the Messiah in the most extreme sense: going well beyond formulaic mimicking, he must, it is stressed, trespass "la Magestad de los cortos limites del nombre" (*Política* 165). Thus the act of representation is summoned to the terrain of the miraculous.

The immediate political pertinence of such an act is made clear through implicit allusion to economic malaise. In effect, the very idea of the king as giving of his own body to redeem his people is an ingenious response to a situation in which Spanish subjects feel themselves sucked dry by the Crown, ruined and starved by the required contributions for war. Building on the precept that the ruler must not bleed his kingdom, which is also exemplified by a story about King John I who refuses all pleasures and insists on mourning because of the pain inflicted on his subjects by necessary tributes (*Política* 184), Quevedo creates a formula through which the king can turn controversy about the cost of the Union of Arms to his own advantage.

As is the case in part I, the distribution of goods is shown to be fundamental to the king's role. But now the king lacks worldly control over this distribution. If initially it was the king who, formidable in his command, demanded that his subjects ask for favor in a humble manner, in part II, he must himself learn to ask. His requests, moreover, are denied. Just as Christ is refused a drink of water by the Samaritan woman at the well, the king's subjects do not willingly grant the king what he needs. Here the criticisms that abounded about Philip IV's lack of political acumen, about his surrendering to the energetic Olivares, are creatively transformed: the ruler emerges as the main repository of divine punishment, offering his body and his blood to his subjects. It is through his status as victim, that the sovereign conserves his exceptionality. The performance of pietas envisaged here is a quintessentially hegemonic gesture, emblematic of the "fetishism" that Bourdieu associates with penitential discourses: "It is in abolishing himself completely in favor of God or the People that the priest turns himself into God or the People. It is when I become Nothing—and because I am capable of becoming Nothing, of abolishing myself, of forgetting myself, of sacrificing myself, of dedicating myself—that I become Everything" (*Language* 211).

Conserving Corporeal Supremacy

That the identification between the Habsburg king and Christ was reinforced, beyond artistic programs, in the realm of social protocol, is well attested to in Corpus Christi processions, where the sovereign played a leading role, walking directly behind the conveyance that carried the monstrance (Paterson 16). The most conspicuous example, though, was a ritual performed the Thursday before Easter, which constituted a veritable imitatio Christi. Breaking with his customary withdrawal from direct contact with the public, the monarch would wash the feet of thirty paupers in commemoration of Jesus's washing his apostles' feet, as recorded in the Gospel of John. There would follow a meal which the king himself served to his humble guests (Kléber Monod 135).

The association with Christ's sacrifice, furthermore, can also be said to condition the king's personal sense of self outside the world of ceremony, as is demonstrated by Philip IV's decision in 1642 to go to Aragon in order to be near the troops in the war with France, against the advice of his councils. In an attempt to rally loyalty and boost recruitment, the king abandons the lavish Madrid court and its entertainments for a modest hunting lodge in Zaragoza, exposing himself to the rigors of proximity to death and disease resulting from the nearby battles. More revealing still are his intimate expressions of humility, a constant of his correspondence with Sor María Agreda, which lasted from 1643, when they first met, to the year of their deaths (both of them died in 1665). Continually thanking the nun, who was herself utterly inexperienced in affairs of government, for the solace of her pious words, Philip IV devoutly mourns the unending succession of military defeats. Answering Sor María's recommendations that he combat geopolitical problems with religious fervor—at issue specifically is the failure of the king's negotiations for peace with the rest of Europe and his vulnerability to Turkish invasions—the king reaffirms his own faith, in a way that recalls the images of martyrdom under discussion:

> Si el fruto de los trabajos es como decís, puede tenerme por muy dichoso padeciéndolos, y quisiera saberlos ofrecer a nuestro Señor como se debe, si bien mi flaqueza temo me lo impide. Los que yo padezco los llevo bien y con aliento, pues todos son más benignos castigos de lo que merezco; pero el ver padecer tantos pobres y tantos inocentes con estas inquietudes y guerras [. . .] me atraviesa el corazón, y si con mi sangre lo pudiera remediar, la empleara de bonísima gana

en ello. Fío de la misericordia de nuestro Señor que se ha de doler de todos y mitigar sus justos castigos; que aunque no lo merecemos, es grande su misericordia. (Torrente Ballester 56)

Yet the tone that emerges here—and the same can be said regarding the king's comportment in the foot-washing ritual—maintains itself within the bounds of conventional decorum. Indeed, the outward display of extreme sentiment is deemed unacceptable because it jeopardizes royal dignity. An unassuming pose is seen as the best reflection of authority. About the very human likenesses of the king produced by the Spanish *pintores del rey,* such as Velázquez, Feros notes they "lacked any symbol that would depict the Spanish king as an absolute and all-powerful ruler that gave enormous authority to this form of royal representation" ("'Sacred'" 86). Such intent to portray the monarch as "virtuous, paternalistic, and benevolent" (Feros, "'Sacred'" 86) is, again, consonant with prevalent contemporary views about royal demeanor. As Juan Márquez counsels in his *El governador christiano,* "Procurara tambien el Principe, que sus palabras vayan templadas de grauedad, y dulçura, y sin ninguna aspereza" (381; see also Rivadeneira 548–49); in other words, the legitimacy of the king's power depends on his abstention from deliberately usurping it.

From this perspective, the degree to which Quevedo's particular representation of *humilitas* infringes established boundaries becomes all the more obvious. This is made clear in his citation of a biblical passage, also included in part I, in which Judas protests against Mary's anointing of the Messiah's body with perfume. Quevedo accuses the disciple of cheapening authority by proposing that the perfume be sold: "Que Iudas fue Arbitrista, y que el suyo fue arbitrio, ya se vè, pues sus palabras fueron, que se podia vender el vnguento, y darse a los pobres" (*Política* 182). "Arbitrios" are considered equivalent to stealing because they take away from one person to give to another. Accordingly, the traitor's proposition is deemed blasphemous, given the untransferable nature of Christ's authority. The supremacy of his body must be maintained at all costs.

It is by now a commonplace to say that politics is instrumentalized not just through the overt imposition of force, but also through the capturing of individual wills. By definition, then, politics is dependent on a certain degree of mystification. According to Clifford Geertz, "A world wholly demystified is a world wholly depoliticized" (qtd. in Kertzer 48). But Quevedo takes this concept to the extreme by erecting a world not somewhat, but wholly mystified. At one level, what we have here is the recipe for a personalized form of absolutist kingship. The mobilization of deep emotion toward the person of the king would be antithetical to the "lien abstrait, quantitative, impersonnel, d'individus serialisés" (Apostolidès, *Le roi-machine* 50) that is the mark of a high degree of institutionalization. Such is the case, offers Apostolidès, with the French court, where the entrenchment of formidable protocol renders the actual person of the king dispensable. He is reduced to pure formality: "Au roi machiniste succède alors un roi-machine dont l'unique corps se confond avec la machine de l'Etat. A la fin du règne, la place du roi devient une case vide, susceptible d'être occupée par quiconque possède la réalité effective du pouvoir" (Apostolidès, *Le roi-machine* 131). Although the Spanish state machine was somewhat less well oiled, contemporaries are certainly aware of the same danger. Already in the time of Philip II, a foreign ambassador famously told His Majesty that he was "nothing but a ceremony" (qtd. in Elliott, "The Court" 142). By combining messianic fervor and otherworldly exceptionality, Quevedo infuses the king's body with a transfixing vitality.

At another level, indissociable from this political recipe, is an aesthetic one. *Política de Dios* is just as much about the power of art as about the power of monarchy. The eucharistic model of social transaction on which the conservation of political order is made to depend is ultimately possible only in a world in which the boundary between art and life has been utterly dissolved. Only then can mimetic representation have the virtual impact embedded in the picture magic described by Gadamer. Quevedo's appropriation of the symbology of the martyred Christ constitutes an attempt to achieve in the political terrain the "methodological priority" that Gadamer assigns to artistic transmission in the philosophical realm (137). Given the energeia with which Quevedo endows regal performance, his envisioned spectacle constitutes a kind of conceptismo put into practice, a conceptismo, however, that seeks not to entertain, nor to seduce, but to inspire awe and fear. But we cannot consider the high-stakes rhetorical performance formulated in *Política de Dios* in isolation from Quevedo's reflections about the political decline of the word. These will be the subject of the following chapters.

THE AGONISTIC WORD

One day took away the glory of an age, and struck by grief
The eloquence of the Latin tongue grew dumb with sadness.
Once the sole guard and saviour of the distressed,
Always the glorious leader of his country, champion
Of the senate, bar, laws, ritual, civil life,
Voice of the public—now silenced for ever by cruel arms.
—Seneca the Elder, *Suasoriae*

To what class of things do the words which rhetoric uses relate?
—Plato, *Gorgias*

DISPLAYED IN THE ELEVENTH CHAPTER of Saavedra Fajardo's *Empresas políticas* is an emblem depicting a broken bell with the inscription "Ex Pvlsv Noscitvr," that is, "Known by Its Ring" (278).[1] The lesson to be drawn here is that the king must carefully choose his words, for, like the bell, they can be heard from afar and hence are bound to be interpreted or misinterpreted in many different ways: "Ninguna palabra suya se cae al que las oye. Fijas quedan en la memoria, y pasan luego de unos a otros por un examen riguroso, dándoles cada uno diferentes sentidos. [. . .] Porque las palabras de los reyes son los principales instrumentos de reinar. En ellas están la vida o la muerte; la honra o la deshonra; el mal o el bien de sus vasallos. [. . .] No hay palabra del príncipe que no tenga su efecto" (Saavedra Fajardo, *Empresas* 279–80). A similar reflection on the extensive reach of the king's words is to be found in Tommaso Roccabella's *Prencipe deliberante* (translated into Spanish as *El príncipe deliberante* by Sebastián de Ucedo): "La lengua pequeña parte del hombre, es un Magistrado supremo, por cuyo medio comparte la fama las alabanças del hombre, ò el mal blazon, que agraua la que desmerece" (114). This vital connection between speech and reputación, itself considered central to the success of government, was a commonplace of rulership literature.

Quevedo shared the view that *fama* could make or break a ruler, but his treatment of the topic significantly differs from that of other anti-Machiavellians, who tended to emphasize the crucial role of prudence in the construction of public image (Rivadeneira 525; Santa María 174; Fernández Santamaría 77–123; Bireley 82). In *Marco Bruto,* the preoccupation that the ruler should be vigilant of what he says is in large measure outweighed by the worry that his voice has lost its ring. The contrast made apparent in the work, between the silent early modern king and the spirited Roman rhetor draws our attention to the potential challenges of conserving heroic models of political speech in a pragmatic age.[2] Like *Política de Dios, Marco Bruto* vindicates a body-centered poetics predicated on the notion of unmediated contact between speaker and audience. At the same time, appropriating late antique discourses on the decline of eloquence, it concerns itself with the plummeting of oratorical ideals in its own epoch.

Reminiscent of collected and often illustrated vignettes of celebrated figures, such as Francisco Pacheco's *Libro de descripción de verdaderos retratos de ilustres y memorables varones* (1599), Francisco Gómez de Reguera's *Empresas de los reyes de Castilla y de León* (1632), and Hernando del Pulgar's *Claros varones de Castilla* (1486), *Marco Bruto* prefaces the summary of the hero's life and achievements, which constitutes the first part of the work, with the description of a medal bearing Brutus's portrait. The reverse of the medal reads, "Entre los dos puñales el pileo o birrete, insignia de la libertad, y abajo en los idus de marzo la fecha del día en que dió la muerte a César" (Quevedo, *Marco* 920). Quevedo further elaborates this ekphrastic presentation by adding a Ciceronian sententia: "'Haces mención de Epicuro, y atréveste a decir: *el varón sabio no se ha de encargar de la república*. ¿No te espanta esta proposición el ceñuelo de nuestro Bruto?'" (*Marco* 920). With mention of Caesar's assassination and a question challenging the premise that a wise man cannot take charge of the republic, along with reference to Brutus's fearsome gaze, Quevedo welds image, device, and saying into a symbol of long-lasting public glory. He turns to the republican rhetor not for his political principles, which are antithetical to his own ultra-absolutist beliefs, but because, in possession of immediate control over the audience, the illustrious Roman embodies a form of transmission that has been lost in the modern political arena.

In Quevedo's era, rhetoric is certainly a central part of the social fabric, having a prominent role in school curricula and displaying itself in epistolary production or in venues such as cultivated conversation or formal competitions (López Grigera 17; Fumaroli 138). And yet there was no secular political forum for epideictic oratory, as there had been in republican

Rome. Inspired public speech of the kind that sought to lead its listeners to action was, above all, confined to the pulpit. In the institutional political sphere, information and discussion circulated through written memoranda. The spoken word was, of course, employed in some contexts, such as council meetings or private audiences between the king and a subject asking for a particular benefit. But these venues were highly formalized, leaving little room for extensive dialogue or monologue (Rodríguez Villa 111–12). Against this framework, *Marco Bruto* functions as a critical reflection not just on royal communication, but also on the general state of secular eloquence and its perceived loss of direction. Revisiting Latin preoccupations about the banalization of rhetoric under empire, Quevedo attempts to resist what he regards as the descent of the word to social inconsequence and trifling entertainment. In so doing, he underlines the discontinuities between traditional and emergent cultural practices.

Renaissance grammarians and literary theorists once urged men of letters to infuse the Spanish language with the grandeur of Latin and the mellifluence of Tuscan. They saw stylistic magnificence, embodied in an aesthetics of abundance, variety, richness, and decorum, as a projection of empire building (Gauger 50). Hence Fernando de Herrera called on Spanish poets to emulate the refinement of Ciceronian and Petrarchan traditions and rescue Castilian from its entrenched ascetic rusticity (138). The ultimate measure of civilized existence, linguistic adornment was viewed as a necessary complement to Spain's newly consolidated geopolitical hegemony (Herrera 151). Echoed here is the spirit of Antonio de Nebrija's grammatical enterprise that had been formulated as a means to guarantee Spain its righteous universal stature. "The key to Nebrija's concept of history," explains Ignacio Navarrete, "is his notion that Castile is at a pivotal instant, which he links typologically to the rule of Solomon in Israel, Alexander in Greece, and Augustus in Rome. Not all nations achieve this moment, and it has literally moved westward and arrived in Spain" (23).

If already in Nebrija's triumphal conception of language, the potential tension between the sedentary cultivation of letters and military expansionism did not go unnoticed (Navarrete 24), in subsequent centuries, the awareness of this conflict would become ever more pronounced. With the decline of Spain's geopolitical and economic fortunes and the accompanying transformations in worldview being felt across Europe, the inherently civic function and social power of language ceased to be taken for granted. Belief in an expanded linguistic hegemony, so apparent in Nebrija's promotion of the printing press and of foreign study of Spanish (Navarrete 23–24), became compromised by rapidly growing skepticism about the possibility of fruitful communication. Although the influence of Petrus Ramus in Spain tends to be minimized (Ong, *Ramus* 305), he did, in fact, mark Spanish letters (Fernández López 143–44). Clearly, Spain was not immune from the kinds of tensions that elsewhere, most notably in Protestant Europe, led to a curricular reshuffling.[3] Ramus's denying of "any oral or aural" (Ong, *Ramus* 289) components to dialectic and his explicit differentiation between speech and rigorous thought in many ways ran counter to Tridentine icon- and performance-oriented cultural programs. Yet the distrust of rhetoric that elsewhere marked a move toward scientific logic also made itself felt in Spain, although, of course, with a different set of implications. Writing of the intellectual turn behind the Ramist legacy, Walter Ong observes, "The attitude toward speech has changed. Speech is no longer a medium in which the human mind and sensibility lives. It is resented, rather, as an accretion to thought, hereupon imagined as ranging noiseless concepts or 'ideas' in a silent field of mental space. Here the perfect rhetoric would be to have no rhetoric at all. Thought becomes a private, or even an antisocial enterprise" (*Ramus* 291). In many senses, Quevedo is operating in a milieu averse to this scheme, given its continued conception of language as a vehicle of active indoctrination and social fashioning. But the shortcomings of this performative model are quite evident from within. Quevedo and his compatriots would have been well aware of the danger that speech could become an "accretion."

From the regular denunciation of preachers for pandering to audience passions (Smith 25), to the outcries against the stylistic license of cultista poets (Jáuregui 71), to the concerns about the slippery nature of speech in political literature, posthumanist Spain sees a generalized distrust in the word, among the salient symptoms of the ideological, intellectual, and theological rifts of Reform and Counter-Reform. In a framework where the listener is always a potential enemy, classical definitions of communication as resting on shared values give way to the more sinuous standards of astute manipulation. The humanist celebration of man's ability to assume countless roles must forcibly change in a world where political and social action are accommodated to the demands of reason of state (Fernández Santamaría 134). Whereas, in Juan Luis Vives's "Fabula de homine (1518)," the ability to fabricate illusion is a measure of human divinity and harmonious sociability, in Quevedo's more skeptical era, illusionism is fraught with problematic connotations. Although artfulness continues to be touted as a social and cultural necessity, the dangers of such image-centeredness provoke some worries, as is eloquently illustrated by one of the main characters of Calderón de la Barca's *El médico de su honra*.

Alluding to her jeopardized honor, doña Leonor says, "En secreto quisiera más perdella, / que con público escándalo tenella" (Calderón de la Barca, *El médico* 106). Such formulations of the elusive task of avoiding misinterpretation and controlling public image are, in effect, a constant of the stage. They are yet one more example of the tension-ridden coexistence of outward performance as primordial determinant of individual value and the awareness of its volatile condition.

It is no coincidence that Saavedra Fajardo warns that the king must be guarded in his speech, for reputación is built as much on withholding information as it is on issuing it. In fact, one could go so far as to say that the value of eloquence is undercut by the awareness of the need for the timely practice of silence. Tacitean secrecy gains firm ground in the realm of the civil servant and the domesticated urban nobility who must contend with private intrigue. In his *Teatro monárquico de España,* Pedro Portocarrero y Guzmán would, quite significantly, devote an entire chapter to lauding the virtues of silence:

> Es el silencio la sal que sazona todos los negocios grandes. Es el que asegura el logro de las resoluciones. En él suele consistir el aumentarse con gran gloria una monarquía o perderse con una infamia. El silencio es el vínculo y la seguridad de todo lo que se trata y dispone. Si éste no se halla en la boca de los ministros, no puede haber seguridad en las repúblicas. Si sus magistrados y consejos no son observantísimos en este punto, todo se perderá. La obligación de éstos es guardar secreto y la del príncipe darles buen ejemplo. (278)

Such expressions of the need to curb the passions attest to a nascent political rationalism: "Against the desire for self-aggrandizement, [early modern writers] opposed the desire for self-preservation or fear of violent death" (Kahn and Saccamano 3). But if, at some levels, the quest for glory is displaced by an emphasis on institutional conservation, it is also fair to say that the Spanish anti-Machiavellians by no means abandoned age-old models of excellence. Rather, they adapted them to the complex needs of a new world order.

Unlike his compatriots, who reconcile Tacitean discretion and Christian norms, Quevedo polarizes them, thereby subverting the ideological accommodations that lie at the core of the Counter-Reformation imaginary (Tierno Galván 42, 72; Malvezzi 98; Bireley). In his substantive study of early modern Spanish political thought, José Fernández Santamaría points out, "Quizá caso único entre sus contemporáneos, Quevedo insiste machaconamente que cristianismo y razón de Estado son antitéticos" (55). Just as the second part of *Política de Dios* promotes the pathos-ridden charisma of the beleaguered Christ king, *Marco Bruto* exalts a poetics of brashness embodied by the embattled orator. In doing so, the text reflects the shifting nature of virtù in an epoch when this concept has come to be defined as the capacity to properly manage adversity. Whereas his contemporaries stop short of opposing this more elastic virtù to traditional Aristotelian or Catholic political ethics, linking it to prudence, which, in turn, they hail as a core moral obligation (Zevallos 97; Campanella 67), Quevedo refuses such compromises. He dissociates virtù from politic calculation, but without returning to the Erasmian conflation of the good ruler and the good man (Erasmus, *The Education* 51). His is not, then, an idealist reaction against moral relativism, but rather, as we shall see, a stylistic recourse for endowing the word with the definitiveness of the *fiat lux*.

Taking to an extreme Senecan models of virility that tended to be bound up with courtly discretion, the oratorical exempla presented in *Marco Bruto* contain a degree of vehemence that goes against the grain of rationalized restraint. As noted in chapter 1, Roger Chartier would read the absolutist state's symbolic production as reflecting the containment of violence that brought the feudal age to a close (*On the Edge* 96). Defying such control and rebelling against the domestication of letters, Quevedo reaches back to the originary violence of the historical process. Only there, in his view, only in the stir of momentous confrontation can that which "transcends the human" be found (Longinus 183; see also Forcione, *Majesty* 162–65, 180). But before going any further with this argument, let us devote some exclusive attention to the layered structure of *Marco Bruto*.

"Tres Muertes en una Vida": The Shape of the Work

The tripartite organization of *Marco Bruto* and its different dates of production are subjects unto themselves and thus require a brief introduction. The text is a composite work that was written over the course of thirteen years (1631–44), parts I and II having been drafted in the early 1630s and part III having been added after 1643. Part I, which narrates Brutus's rise to power and his assassination of Caesar, takes the form of an annotated translation of Plutarch's *Parallel Lives*. Each translated passage is followed by Quevedo's exegesis of the event at issue. Part II, included as an example of how the lessons learned from the famed conspiracy are of continued relevance to contemporary politics, comprises the transcription of and commentary on the letters exchanged between Fernando el Católico and the mayor of the fortress of La Peza, Francisco Pérez de Barradas, in 1515. In his first *instrucción,* Fernando asks Barradas to detain certain vessels come to Málaga to take Grand Captain Gonzalo Fernández de Córdoba to Italy or France, where he would supposedly take part in a conspiracy against the king. Although Pérez de Barradas responds that he has found no trace of the conspirators, Fernando presses him, in a second letter, to conduct his search more aggressively. The reader is thereby led to compare the conduct of the early modern ruler with that of the ancient leader and, accordingly, to evaluate Fernando's handling of the conspiracy against him. Also at issue, as will be made clear, are the vindication of the performative flair exhibited by Caesar and Brutus and the indictment of the bureaucratic king's uninspired expression. Finally, in part III, the aftermath of Brutus's conspiracy is discussed through an assortment of Seneca the Elder's *suasoriae.* The rhetorical competition concludes with a retelling of Cicero's violent death at the hands of Mark Antony's envoy.

As is the case with *Política de Dios,* with whose dates it overlaps, *Marco Bruto* reflects the changes in Quevedo's political career that took him from palace favorite to outcast.[4] Something can surely be made of the fact that the first two parts, which expound upon rulership and conspiracy, were initially written between 1631 and 1632, when Quevedo was still working for Olivares, whereas part III, which portrays Cicero's death, was added in 1644 after Quevedo's imprisonment. It stands to reason that, in the first case, Quevedo still holds some apparent belief in the public role of eloquence, whereas, in the second, irrevocably disillusioned as he was at this point with the centers of power, he makes the tenuous position of great speech ever more apparent. The implicit parallels between Cicero's plight and that of Quevedo, himself a victim of conspiracy charges, are evident. No doubt, in Quevedo's mind, they were proof that the ancient Roman despondence about a political culture that was losing muscle was altogether applicable in his own day.

But of chief importance here is the fact that beyond the generic and thematic differences between the three parts, all of them treat rhetorical performance as an ultimate political end.[5] In his introduction, Quevedo plainly identifies his work with the realm of oral communication and social modeling: "No escribo historia, sino discurso con tres muertes en una vida, que a quien supiere leerlas darán muchas vidas en cada muerte" (*Marco* 921). Opposed to an individualized model of reading and interpretation, he links the reception of the text metaphorically to a live performative framework. As has been made clear in previous chapters, the survival of oral and performative principles within print culture continues to be ubiquitous. This is so in epistolary production, in poetry, and in fictional prose. From Justus Lipsius's assertion that the well-written epistle brings the distant correspondent to life to Gracián's notion that the poetic conceit must be infused with life and soul, to the life of don Quijote within *Don Quijote,* imagined as a dialogue in progress, examples of the conception of texts as direct oral exchange are plentiful.

What is distinctly notable in Quevedo's case, I would contend, is the inordinate defensiveness of body-centered communication, as though he found it necessary to take drastic steps to ensure its survival in the world of paper and print. Certainly, criticism of printed matter was common at the time, as mentioned in chapter 1. Yet this unease was, for the most part, registered in satires or other grievance literature, whereas, in Quevedo's oeuvre, it becomes a motif of ubiquitous import in all forms of discourse and has a determinant role in his political theory in a way that is not generally characteristic of anti-Machiavellian treatises. In short, Quevedo's lugubrious perception of material cultural change strongly marks his rhetorical philosophy and praxis.

In *Marco Bruto,* Quevedo's reactive stance is reflected in the emphatic display of aggression on which the survival of effective eloquence seemingly depends. Unlike his fellow men of letters, who find a new creative potential for ingenio in the modern world of the discreto, Quevedo sees its powers rekindled only in the rawer arena of transgressive confrontation. As I shall show in the following section, he gives Lipsian ideals on letter writing a particularly dramatic turn, constructing models of fortitude that clash with other, more civically-minded interpretations of political being.

The Paper King

That Quevedo is writing in the era of the "rey papelero" is made clear at the start of the second part of *Marco Bruto,* when he refers to the documents he has in his hand: "Hallé esta noticia mirando para otros fines los papeles de los grandes servicios de la casa muy ilustre de don Fernando de Barradas, que él tiene en su poder, originales de mano del rey Católico; y trasladados por mí con toda fidelidad, son los que se siguen" (973). In other words, we are a far cry from the republican stage, on which political leaders perform in the flesh. Instead of the resounding voice of the ruler, we have before us his punctiliously redacted prose faithfully transcribed by the writer, who nevertheless yearns for the performative energeia associated with the "warrior king" (Elliott, *Imperial Spain* 170).

Quevedo's criticism of Fernando's detailed instructions on how the mayor of La Peza should proceed to catch the conspirators is harsh, suggesting as it does the king's utter lack of authority: "Lo mismo es publicar un príncipe que tiene entre sus vasallos muchos traidores, que confesar un hombre que tiene muchas enfermedades incurables y ninguna salud; y con la codicia que a éste le espían los herederos, al otro le atiende la malicia alborozada de los enemigos" (*Marco* 977). The denunciation has not so much to do with what Fernando does, as with how he does it. Indeed, Quevedo's positions about what course of action to take against conspiracy change from work to work and even within a single work. In the second part of *Política de Dios,* for instance, the king is applauded for forgiving his enemy, whereas, in the first part of *Marco Bruto,* Caesar is criticized for not taking the proper steps to stop his traitors. Meanwhile, in the second part, the Roman leader emerges as far superior to the Catholic king not because of his pragmatism or his prudence—he is lacking in both—but because of his capacity to emotionally engage his audience: "En la cabeza de Pompeyo los hizo reír con lágrimas" (Quevedo, *Marco* 979).

To gain further understanding of this argument it is helpful to consider an earlier document: Quevedo's 1621 transcription of and commentary on the letter from don Fernando el Católico to the first viceroy of Naples. The letter commands the viceroy to punish the envoy sent to announce the pope's intention to intrude upon monarchical jurisdiction. In the accompanying analysis, Quevedo upholds the sovereign for his forceful response, which, he says, is antithetical to the conduct of "los políticos de la comodidad, que llaman reputación y prudencia lo que es sufrimiento y poltronería" ("Carta" 789). Commenting on the style of Fernando's correspondence, he says, "Es de notar que, como carta de mano del Rey, es todo fuego, y no se conoce en ella el apocamiento de las civilidades con que algunos secretarios afeminan lo robusto del discurso de los grandes reyes" ("Carta" 791). The sovereign's writing is turned into an epitome of masculine forcefulness, endowed with the furor of forum and battlefield, a deliberate distinction being made between it and the feminized unvaliant prose of the secretary.

On a general level, this predilection for a direct and spirited form of address is a reflection of epochal trends. Although there are relatively few manuals on epistolary rhetoric produced in early modern Spain, it is safe to say that letter writing served as a key venue for accumulating and displaying social capital (Bouza, *Corre*). I mention the phenomenon in passing because it shows that the written word conserves the function of immediate interpersonal exchange assigned to it by Justus Lipsius, who, quoting Turpilius, would say that letter writing "'makes the absent present'" (9). At the start of his brief manual on epistolary content and style, Lipsius does acknowledge that this practice replaces direct address, pointing out that it became customary in the time of Caesar, "who was 'first to devise the procedure of conferring with friends by letters, when either his affairs or the size of the city would not always give him the opportunity for personal meetings'" (9). However, he goes on to stress that such texts preserve the spirit of unmediated contact, as demonstrated by the Senecan epistle that he cites: "I see you, my Lucilius; what is more, I hear you. Truly, I am so much with you that I wonder whether I ought to begin to write you not letters but rather memoranda" (qtd. in Lipsius 9). That such an attribution of praesentia to correspondence would have become common currency among Quevedo's compatriots is obvious from Saavedra Fajardo's envisioning bureaucratic documents as a seamless bonding between correspondents. Characterizing the secretary as "una mano de la voluntad del príncipe" (*Empresas* 659), he goes on to develop a complex metaphor intertwining the person of the king with the administrative machine. The secretary's pen "es también compás; porque no sólo ha de escribir, sino medir y ajustar las resoluciones, compasar las ocasiones y los tiempos, para que ni lleguen antes ni después las ejecuciones" (Saavedra Fajardo, *Empresas* 659).

Beyond its investment in personalized communication, this conception of emergent bureaucratic culture shows marked differences vis-à-vis Quevedo's. Where the mainstream mirrors of princes attempt to express the expanding administrative apparatus as continuous with age-old schemes of organic leadership (de la Torre 57, 62; Santa María 18, 39, 42; Portocarrero y Guzmán 313–14), Quevedo disputes such smooth transitions. As his attack on the pusillanimous femininity of the secretary implies, he considers heroic only those actions which accumulate aura in a single person, actions, that is, that go against the spirit of an institutionalized division of labor. Building on a Senecan gendering of virtù, he ties effective communication to an exclusively virile forcefulness. "Man's speech is just like his life," Seneca would write in a letter to Lucilius devoted to style:

> Exactly as each individual man's actions seem to speak, so people's style of speaking often reproduces the general character of the time. [. . .]

Wantonness in speech is proof of public luxury, if it is popular and fashionable, and not confined to one or two individual instances. A man's ability cannot possibly be of one sort and his soul of another. If his soul be wholesome, well-ordered, serious, and restrained, his ability also is sound and sober. Conversely, when the one degenerates, the other is also contaminated. Do you not see that if a man's soul has become sluggish, his limbs drag and his feet move indolently? If it is womanish, that one can detect the effeminacy by his very gait? That a keen and confident soul quickens the step? (*Seneca ad Lucilium* 301–3)

That the style makes the man is an ongoing premise of Quevedo's oeuvre, as is the direct, if unexplained, connection assumed between masculinity, vigor, and virtue, on the one hand, and effeminacy, delicacy, and social torpor, on the other. Such physiological profiling is noticeable in much of Quevedo's diagnosis of cultural and political malaise, which arbitrarily assigns moral laxity to any form of communication that is not directly combative. Symptomatic in this sense are his *Premáticas,* whose denunciations of poets, preachers, and commoners for their hackneyed verbal expression are ridden with allusions to physical and social degeneracy (*Prosa* 320–21). Among the most strident of these is his mock pronouncement against practitioners of the conceit: "Habiendo considerado que esta infernal seta de hombres condenados a perpetuo concepto, despedazadores y tahúres de vocablos, han pegado la dicha roña de poesía a las mujeres, declaramos que nos damos por desquitados con este mal que les han hecho del que nos hicieron en Adán" (*Prosa* 186). Quevedo describes their lack of verbal restraint as a foul infection that spreads throughout the social body.

Pitting itself against such social malignancy, his portrayal of Marcus Brutus writing in the midst of battle preparations and his subsequent reevaluations of Brutus's character exemplify the extent to which Quevedo revives the spectacular facet of the Senecan program:

En el ejército, Marco Bruto, fuera del estudio y la lección, sólo gastaba las horas que forzosamente asistía a Pompeyo. Y no sólo se ocupó en escribir y leer en el tiempo desocupado; mas siendo la sazón más ardiente del verano, en el más encendido crecimiento del día, cuando en la guerra Farsálica, estando impedidos los escuadrones en lagunas y pantanos, fatigado de la hambre y de la siesta, por no haberle sus criados traído la tienda ni el refresco; y cuando todos (por haberse de dar la batalla a otro día) estaban o temerosos del suceso, o solícitos

> de su mejor defensa, Marco Bruto toda la noche gastó en escribir un compendio de Polibio, ilustrado con sus advertencias. (*Marco* 927)

In strong contrast with the cautious early modern monarch working at his desk, the Roman hero is touched with exceptional inspiration. The stuff of legend, the act of writing is presented here as an extension of a military feat. Therein lies the essence of Brutus's power to mobilize the conspirators. Such is the authority exuded by his presence that Caesar himself does not attempt to stop the conspiracy, despite his suspicions. Revealing, indeed, is Caesar's comment on Brutus's oration convincing him to be reconciled with his enemies, Cassius and the African King Juba: "Este mozo no sé lo que quiere; pero lo que quiere lo quiere con vehemencia" (Quevedo, *Marco* 929). It is not Brutus's ability to genuinely persuade that is commemorated. On the contrary, his greatness stems from the fact that he affects people's decisions, beyond and sometimes even despite their better judgment.

Explicitly alluding to his hero's lack of ethical probity toward the beginning of *Marco Bruto,* Quevedo brands Brutus a "mal leal," whereas Caesar is a "buen tirano" (920). He also discredits the conspirator's political convictions since, according to Quevedo's staunchly monarchical stance, all power should be consolidated in one ruler: "Son tiranos los senados en las repúblicas, y tiranos multiplicados" (971). Brutus failed even in relation to his own agenda, Quevedo points out, for the republic was not restored. Indeed, that he authorized Mark Antony to influence public opinion was nothing short of foolish: "Marco Antonio sabía ejecutar bien lo que pensaba mal, y Marco Bruto ejecutaba mal lo que pensaba bien" (Quevedo, *Marco* 969). Summing up Brutus's achievements retrospectively, Quevedo concludes, "¿Qué cosa más [. . .] admirable que sus estudios, más docta que sus oraciones, más reverenciada que sus costumbres, más interesada que sus gobiernos, y más valerosa que su persona? Esto al principio; mas al fin, cuando se llegó a la ejecución de sus designios, ¿qué cosa más bruta ni más tonta se puede considerar que Marco Bruto?" (*Marco* 970).

For Seneca, effective speech and demeanor were a direct extension of a "well-ordered soul." But, in Quevedo's scheme, virtue is no longer the product of a Platonic harmony in which reason governs the passions. Instead, virtue is something of a chimerical façade that exhibits itself with overwhelming persuasiveness, only to disappear without generating substantive change. In this sense, the principle of *constantia* is betrayed. Thus, although voicing a critique of moral relativism, Quevedo's version of excellence is itself quintessentially spectacular, making up as it does for the absence of moral absolutes with the compelling presence of sensation so vehemently communicated that it violates the parameters of ingenio as a civically defined social practice.

Reformulating the *Vir Bonus*

To more specifically define how Quevedean heroism diverges from other contemporary definitions of social grandeur, we should attend to the increased emphasis that post-Tridentine rhetorical theories place on exceptional ingenuity. As Christian Mouchel points out, the Renaissance standard of "iudicium" gradually gives way to that of "la hauteur d'inspiration et de la magnanimité" (454) as a guiding rhetorical principle. In Spain as in the rest of Europe, Longinus's treatise *On the Sublime,* edited in 1555 by Paolo Manuzio, gains currency (López Grigera 80). Formulated there is an aesthetics of the extraordinary, particularly relevant to a period so aware of its instrumental value. Longinus holds that "preeminence" supersedes "correctness" (184), an idea that accords perfectly with the epochal preference for natural brilliance over a learned command of rules, the former being considered an indispensable guarantor of communicative superiority. Here the difference between natural and learned magnificence must be understood metaphorically as a reference to the quality of the composition; that the best oratory requires training is not in dispute. Paradoxically, the perfect mastery of this art is charged with the appearance of being the uncontrived product of superlative inspiration. Accordingly, the task of the courtier is to evince greatness, just as it is the priest's duty to evince a glorified religiosity. Oft cited and embroidered upon in this regard is Augustine's assertion that the good preacher must *embody* his interpretation of the Gospels in such a way as to transport his flock (*On Christian* 119).

Definitions of what precisely constitutes exceptional style are not monolithic, as is evident from the marked differences between the excessive ornamental flourish of a Góngora or Paravicino and the dense *brevitas* championed by Gracián and Quevedo. In the latter case, the definition of excellence is informed by a strong regard for efficacy, also a central aim of Senecan laconism and of anti-Ciceronian currents, of which the seventeenth-century cult of brevitas is a central manifestation (López Grigera 9). "Aunque Cicerón boluiera a Púlpito," says Gonzalo Pérez de Ledesma, "pocos tuuieran paciencia para oírle vna hora de preámbulos y tres de oración; y, assí, avría de ceñirse más, si quisiera dezir algo en vna hora, que es lo que sufre oir la más flemática atención" (115). But even among those who find fault with the excesses of the *stilo fiorito,* bluntness is considered equally objectionable.

In his authoritative *Instructiones praedicationis verbi Dei,* which set the oratorical agenda for the Society of Jesus, Carlo Borromeo promotes the notion that faith is mobilized through living embodiment and testimony rather than through textual citation. Yet Borromeo also underlines the need for a certain flourish: "Le prédicateur, par sa parole et la figure que compose sa personne tout entière, n'est plus qu'un état de l'âme, une 'image spirituelle' dont l'intensité emporte l'adhésion du public. Comme objectivation d'une méditation passionnée, son discours doit en demeurer le miroir et le serviteur. D'où la définition d'une juste mesure, moyen terme entre deux extrêmes également défectueux: la suavité et le pathétique affecté, d'une part, la simplicité rugueuse et negligée, d'autre part" (Mouchel 433–34). Juan de Jáuregui y Aguilar touts a similar equilibrium in the realm of poetic composition, criticizing Gongorism for its opaque ornateness while also defending the desirability of *perspicuitas* over *claritas*: poets are to avoid "furiosa afectación" (71) at all costs, yet it is equally imperative that they differentiate the "sublime" (67) conceit from common speech. Hence the message must be "no tan inmediato y palpable, sino con ciertos resplandores no penetrables a vulgar vista" (Jáuregui 125).

In his *Examen de ingenios,* Juan Huarte de San Juan is yet more receptive to *suavitas,* remarking that, once faith has been established, this quality becomes desirable since the public is increasingly sensitive to its effects. He thus distinguishes the speech of the early preachers and philosophers, which is rough and bare, from the cultivated language of his contemporaries, which exudes "calor y humedad" (439). The Athenians, he points out, must have been well aware of this, to judge by their view of Socrates: "La cual doctrina si alcanzaran los atenienses, no se espantaran tanto de ver un hombre tan sabio como Sócrates y que no supiese hablar; del cual decían los que entendían lo mucho que sabía que sus palabras y sentencias eran como unas cajas de Madera tosca y sin cepillar por defuera, pero, abiertas, había dentro en ellas dibujos y pinturas dignas de admiración" (424). As to Paul's lack of stylistic elegance, Huarte de San Juan reflects the following:

> Porque ser el publicador elocuente y tener mucho ornamento de palabras no convenía, atento que la fuerza de los oradores de aquel tiempo se descubría en que hacían entender al auditorio las cosas falsas por verdaderas. [. . .] El ingenio de san Pablo era apropiado para este ministerio; porque tenía grande entendimiento para defender y

probar, en las sinagogas y en la gentilidad, que Jesucristo era el Mesías prometido en la ley, y que no había que esperar otro ninguno. Y, con esto, era de poca memoria; por donde no pudo saber hablar con ornamento de palabras dulces y sabrosas. Y esto era lo que la publicación del Evangelio había menester. (426–27)

Paul's language is thought to be lacking in memory, a faculty essential to the cultivated rhetorician, whose art, precisely, is founded on the knowledge and mastery of a lengthy tradition of oratorical techniques and tropes.

Word-for-word memorization was a central part of academic curricula, dating back to Augustine's theories on the integral relationship between memory and revelation, according to which memorization both preceded understanding and was instrumental to it. Through rote repetition, the student would eventually succeed in internalizing and appropriating imparted knowledge. In his handbook on catechetical teaching, Augustine emphasizes that it is far more productive to watch and listen when the teacher is actively engaged in the subject than simply to read what is dictated (*The First Catechetical*). Memory is described in the *Confessions* as an extremely intimate space, likened to an ocean in its vastness, depth, and constantly changing nature; it is initially fashioned and nourished through the absorption of externally imposed lessons that are "archived" in this infinite storehouse, to be retrieved and to acquire new meanings as the pupil matures (187, 185). Thus the receptive activity of storing material is the basis for the more active faculty of reinterpretation and transformation.

In Huarte de San Juan's treatise, we come across a similar combination of faculties deemed essential to the successful preacher: "Luego los ingenios que se han de elegir para predicadores son, primeramente, los que juntan grande entendimiento con mucha imaginativa y memoria" (464). Memory and understanding are organically linked to the imagination, where the treatise locates the production of warmth required to envelop the audience in the apostolic experience. This experience is, in turn, dependent on the actual voice of the preacher, which is itself determined by the bodily humors. As in Augustine's scheme, oratorical art is naturalized, although this time with a physiological turn. "La voz abultada y sonora, apacible al auditorio; no áspera, ronca ni delgada," writes Huarte de San Juan. "Y aunque es verdad que esto nace del temperamento del pecho y garganta, y no de la imaginativa, pero es cierto que del mesmo temperamento que nace la buena imaginativa, que es calor, deste mesmo sale la buena voz. Y para el intento que llevamos conviene mucho saber esto, porque los teólogos escolásticos, por ser de frío y seco temperamento, no pueden tener buen órgano de voz, lo cual es gran falta para el púlpito" (445). But where Huarte de San Juan identifies the desired rhetorical "warmth" with polish, some theorists denounce ornamental excess for its supposed coldness (Mouchel 434), another sign of the fluidity of rhetorical philosophies.

At the same time, it is safe to say that the mainstream of those concerned with the practical instrumentality of rhetoric, in church or court, defends the need to maintain the equilibrium mentioned by Mouchel between ornamentation and sobriety. In the prologue to Pérez de Ledesma's *Censura de la elocuencia,* Martín de Lanaja pronounces: "La Oración, bien luzida y adornada con matizes retóricos, es gran medio para introducir en el alma dulcemente saludables desengaños. Al contrario sucede en la Oración tosca y desgreñada, porque con su asqueroso desaliño antes ofende que persuade. No basta que los conceptos de un Sermón sean escogidos y bien fundados si no van assistidos y vestidos de estilo decente" (qtd. in Pérez de Ledesma 37). Taking this principle further, Pérez de Ledesma mourns the loss of aesthetic equilibrium, expressing it, like Huarte de San Juan, in terms of corporeal imbalance:

> Muchos son los males que tienen descolorida, sin neruios y en los güessos la Eclesiástica Eloquencia; pero acudo primero al mayor mal. El que le haze casi incurable prouiene de dos contrarios: demasiada lozanía y triste marchitez; por vnos pierden otros, y esta contradición de humores preuierte al daño de vno lo que se receta al otro. Si se fomenta el bazo con algún abrigo, echa chispas el hígado; y si éste se refrigera, aquél tirita; y aun no es éste el mayor mal, sino que cada vno piensa es el sano y el otro el dañado. Es máxima de la prudencia que se perficione el natural con estudio y arte para que las humanas prendas siruan a lo diuino del Púlpito, pero con humildad de criadas, no sea que desvanecidas vsurpen el lugar de señoras. Ésta que nació regla del acierto la tuerzen diuersos genios a opuestos yerros, nunca más incorregibles que quando se doran con hipocresías de rectitud. Pues los picados de agudos todo lo quieren lleuar a punta de concepto, como de lança; no huelgue palabra, todo sea trabajado a fuerça viua de razón y ingenio. Y dicen que merecen gracias y gloria por ello, pues siruen con todas sus fuerças a lo sagrado. Al contrario los presumidos devotos quanto tiene agudeza les espina; enfurécense como bestias picadas del Tábano en oyendo vno déstos que llaman Tabanillos. [. . .] A todos los comprehende igualmente su enojo o ignorancia, que llaman zelo aunque tenga otros designios. (61)

Pérez de Ledesma's stance is orthodox in its demand that art be an instrument of the pulpit and not a usurper of its divine powers. And yet we find in these words something approaching a modern "science of feelings." In denouncing current rhetorical excesses and defending subtler modes of inducing sentiment, Pérez de Ledesma echoes ideas that were to gain wider adherence over a century later, when Friedrich Schiller would praise aesthetics as a practice whose greatness lay in its inducing virtue in individuals without having the "appearance of compulsion" (129). Something similar occurs in Gracián's theory of ingenio. Expanding traditional conceptions of rhetoric as an instrument of persuasion, Gracián situates language in the wider and more sinuous domain of fashioning civilized affect. Its charge would be not merely to captivate, but also to socialize the audience.

Gracián's treatises prove a particularly productive counterpoint from which to approach the idiosyncrasies of Quevedo's rhetorical philosophy, not only because of their sustained reflections on the instrumentality of the conceit and of an agile brevitas, but also because they are equally preoccupied with the retention of a heroic aura. Gracián is as acutely conscious as Quevedo of the discontinuities between the traditional and the new world orders. Reflecting on the somber image of the absolutist state ciphered in *El criticón,* Forcione affirms that Gracián "can be viewed as one of the last and the most conflicted of the Christian humanist writers of the Renaissance" ("At the Threshold" 4). Although his understanding of his era is still grounded in classical and scholastic conceptions of social being, he is deeply troubled by the awareness of their growing anachronism. In his manuals on rhetoric and on courtly conduct, which are of particular pertinence here, we witness the way in which he crafts cultural selves that adapt to the changed political arena: "His works seek to establish patterns of behavior that help people cope with the rules of an established social order that they do not want to transform but that, in any case, they seek to take advantage of" (Spadaccini and Talens xiii). Whereas Pérez de Ledesma continues to harness his aesthetic theories to Christian humility—conceiving of it as a "humble servant of the pulpit"—Gracián autonomizes discursive practices from their strict definition as a means to an end. His formulation of communication along heroic lines, then, while also positing a continuity between art and life, adheres to principles of civic virtue that invite intersubjectivity.

We would be hard pressed to find a passage of Gracián's writings on language and on conduct that does not concern itself with the display of excellence or, to use his own terms, "the superlative," "the sublime," "the heroic," "the perfect," all of which are strongly reminiscent of Longinus's formulations of the extraordinary. In Gracián's work, classical notions of magnificence reach a remarkable height, "height" being here quite the appropriate word for an oeuvre that constantly lapses into spatial metaphors to illustrate its lofty cultural ambitions. Reflecting his aspirations to the infinite, Gracián sums up the purpose of his manual *El héroe*: "Emprendo formar con un libro enano un varón gigante" (5); for him, astuteness is the means to victory, the way to lord it over ("señorear") all the rest (7). Indeed, in this boundless universe, he imagines every social situation as a potential *aristeia*, from the king's gathering grapes unaware of the audience that watches him in awe to the Portuguese merchant's earning himself a diamond for titillating the sovereign with his unexpected cleverness (*El héroe* 18, 15). Running through these passages is a clear association between *agudeza* and social success. As Mercedes Blanco has said, the cult of agudeza is representative of the early modern conception of conduct codes as guidelines for contending with particular circumstances and affecting the will of others, rather than as philosophies geared toward establishing moral good (529). It is no coincidence that Gracián should tell his readers to think of his treatise as a "razón de estado de ti mismo" (*El héroe* 5).

But, I hasten to reiterate, agudeza is also an art of living, a way not merely of dominating people and circumstances, but also of coexisting gracefully in society. Remembered, on the one hand, for having coined the phrase "lo bueno si breve dos veces bueno" (*Oráculo* 175), Gracián should also be hailed as a defender of subtlety and grace: brevity is not, for him, a formula for transmitting aggression, but rather for containing it. Although he promotes a Senecan reliance on mental prowess, upholding overwhelming swiftness of mind as an essential means for social success and cultural plenitude, he does not imagine ingenio as a cutting force or "lance," to use Pérez de Ledesma's term. Instead, he proposes triumph without mordancy, wit without defiance. Extraordinary control, then, implies skilled negotiation rather than direct confrontation. Gracián clearly stipulates that unguarded virulence signifies a loss of power, a descent from human to brute (*El héroe* 9). The luster of Alexander the Great, for instance, is blemished by his having given in to his passions. Meanwhile, Isabel la Católica reigns supreme, unsurpassed as she is in her decorum, as exemplified by her retiring to an isolated corner of the palace to give birth, allowing herself neither grimace nor sigh (Gracián, *El héroe* 9–10). Such models of heroism are fashioned not for the battlefield, but instead for curial and urban life where ruling the emotions is a way of exhibiting strength.

Thus self-restraint functions as a civilizing mechanism, as a means of ensuring social order. Discretion and subtlety are, in short, the required recipes for a pacified existence. Along with the display of wit, the lucid interpretation of the hearts and minds of others is central to the role of the discreto. The task of winning over *voluntades* involves being attuned to them, for the will of the astute individual must be insinuated rather than demanded. What Gracián proposes, then, is a rather complex two-way process of interpretation. The prudent hero does not coerce his audience: his wishes are subtly conveyed, as opposed to overtly manifested. The more gentle art of persuasion exacts a certain degree of discretion from the interlocutor: Gracián "despises all forms of vulgar communication, and he demands a particular type of reader—an 'aristocrat of the intellect'" (Forcione, "At the Threshold" 4).

In sum, Gracián's defense of decorum—like that of Huarte de San Juan and Pérez de Ledesma—is an attempt to fuse together tact and ostentation, an ideal continuous with the Italian Renaissance principle of *sprezzatura*. Gracián's nuanced definition of artifice coincides with that articulated by Count Ludovico in Baldesar Castiglione's *Book of the Courtier*: "'I have found quite a universal rule which in this matter seems to me valid above all others, and in all human affairs whether in word or deed: and that is to avoid affectation in every way possible as though it were some very rough and dangerous reef; and [. . .] to practice in all things a certain *sprezzatura* (nonchalance), so as to conceal all art and make whatever is done or said appear to be without effort and almost without any thought about it'" (43). Similarly, Gracián warns against the appearance of affectation, which he maligns as "lastre de la grandeza" because it hampers the possibility of a freely flowing esteem: "Es muy libre la estimación, no se sujeta a artificio, mucho menos a violencia" (*El héroe* 35). He equates immoderate artifice to violence—whether physical or verbal he does not say—in the sense that it is an attempt to unduly control the audience.

In the light of Erving Goffman's theories of social fashioning, we might make the generalization that pacified coexistence always involves a degree of naturalized theatricality. What is noteworthy in the early modern theories of eloquence under discussion is that they formulate such artfulness as much more than a rule-based means to an end. Thus, conceiving ingenio as a kind of spontaneously occurring inspiration, Gracián remarks, "No se pueden dar reglas ciertas e infalibles para estas sutiles consecuencias; sola la valentía y vivacidad de un ingenio es bastante para tan extravagante discurrir" (*Agudeza* 2:94). More significant yet is the link between ingenio and beauty and its concomitant distinction from univocal truth: "No se contenta el ingenio con sola la verdad, como el juicio, sino que aspira a la hermosura" (Gracián, *Agudeza* 1:54). Gracián sees beauty as the culminating reflection of freely given or uncommanded sublimity. Conversely, he denounces satire, whose overtly programmatic nature he regards as a lapsed sensibility: "Pero hay también perdidos de ingenio como de bienes, pródigos de agudeza para presas sublimes, tagarotes para las viles águilas. Mordaces y satíricos, que si los crueles se amasaron con sangre, éstos con veneno. En ellos la sutileza, con extraña contrariedad por liviana, abate, sepultándolos en el abismo de un desprecio, en la región del enfado" (*El héroe* 12). Gracián might be said to anticipate modern aesthetics, not because he approaches inventive language as possessing a truth autonomous from other forms of knowledge and social practice, but because, in rethinking the role of artifice in the pacified arena of prudence, he dissociates it from the function of political subjection, thereby allowing for the more elusive interplay of subjectivity.

Drastically different from such paradigms of artful socialization is Quevedo's conception of verbal prowess. One could say that Longinian ideals of the sublime are operative in his work insofar as it defines excellence as that which somehow surpasses established norms or studied craftiness. On the other hand, we are far from a civic notion of magnificence, for the exhibition of extraordinariness is not balanced by attention to the necessities of domesticated coexistence or gracious negotiation. To the contrary, Quevedo considers effective performance and pleasurable interaction antithetical. In the instances of aristeia exemplified in his texts, the hero utterly overwhelms the audience; there is a complete subjection to the aura of the protagonist. As we saw in *Política de Dios,* in his capacities as wily statesman and as martyred scapegoat, the Christ king wields utter power over his subjects, who give themselves up entirely to him. In *Marco Bruto,* the emotions of the crowd are similarly taken hostage.

In a scene whose heavy-handed pathos recalls the Passion episodes represented in *Política de Dios,* Portia requests that her husband reveal the secret that she surmises he has been hiding. Crowning her request with a spectacular exploit, she stabs herself before asking Brutus to unveil his worries, in order to prove to him that she can transcend the limitations of her sex and merit his trust: "Oyóla Bruto, y mezclando sus lágrimas con su sangre, pagó su valentía comunicándola el intento que la callaba y de justicia debía a su muerte" (Quevedo, *Marco* 948). Although in a political context starkly different from that of *Política de Dios,* the scene nears a sacramental conception of communication, the authority of speech being demonstrated through bleeding flesh. Supremely effective, the act draws the confession from Brutus's lips.

Also epitomizing this kind of oratorical feat is Mark Antony's speech over Caesar's dead body: "Hoy no es día de hablar de Julio César, sino de enseñarle. Mejor os informarán vuestros ojos de sus heridas que mi lengua. Oíd a su cuerpo, que sus crueles puñaladas tienen voz, y os persuadirán mejor, abiertas con puñales de sus parientes, que mi boca cerrada con los suspiros y anegada con el llanto" (Quevedo, *Marco* 966). The orator has come not to talk, but to show, since Caesar's wounds speak for themselves. Antony in this sense situates himself in a realm beyond argument, for the only possible verdict, it is implied, is engraved on the evidence of the crime. The crowd hastens to carry out what emerges from the speech as an inevitable and natural reaction: revenge. At the sight of the bloodied toga held up by Antony, the masses break out in fury, setting fire to public buildings and to the houses of the conspirators.

Where his contemporaries reject oratorical virulence as something that jeopardizes both individual and community, Quevedo embraces the untrammeled passions of the demagogue as a central social force. Although, of course, Portia's suicidal oratory sets a tone very different from that of the rabble-rouser, it departs just as radically from notions of civility and self-preservation. Both figures, in a sense, attest to the impossibility of language's serving a social function through anything other than extreme exertion. In contrast to Chaïm Perelman's balanced definition of rhetoric as communication directed both to the intellect and to the emotions of the audience, the orators depicted by Quevedo operate purely in the realm of the emotions. Persuasion is thereby reduced to coercion. We have veered away entirely from the logic of seduction premised upon the idea that consensus can be built through the freer appeal to pleasure and rationality.

We are well accustomed to thinking of the satirical Quevedo as the kind of "tabanillo" so maligned by Pérez de Ledesma. But it is especially revealing to note the extent to which Quevedo's conception of the pen and the tongue as a lance extends outside of his satirical corpus. Even when he is at his most civic, in his 1629 letter on the poetry of Fray Luis de León, Quevedo's predilection for forcefulness is clear. Written at a highpoint of his political career, the "Dedicatoria al Excelentísimo señor Conde-Duque" is addressed to Olivares, presenting him with the accompanying collection of poetry. Appropriately, given that the letter speaks to a great statesman, Quevedo exalts Fray Luis from the standpoint of Quintilianic principles of prudence ("Dedicatoria" 46). He underlines the fact that the poet's adhesion to the rules of decorum—"El arte es acomodar la locución al sujeto" ("Dedicatoria" 47)—is an expression of genuine civic virtue. Defining decorum as clarity and sobriety, Quevedo characteristically links it directly to the domain of active performance. He holds up the austerity of Fray Luis's verses as a mirror of Olivares's rhetorical virtues, which he views as instigating action: "Escribió V.E. otra carta, que imprimió el duque de Carpiñano, donde con las dudas enseña y con las preguntas reprehende los halagos que desecha; y pidiendo V.E. advertimientos para la tolerancia de lo molesto en las audiencias, enseñó al autor lo que debió escribir y lo que pudo escusar, sin afectación ni dificultades, enseñando juntamente a escribir y a obrar" (Quevedo, "Dedicatoria" 42).

Needless to say, Quevedo's commentary on Fray Luis's works serves as a pretext for seeking contact with the court.[6] The connection between the Augustinian's classical poetics and the count-duke's politically efficacious prose is more a crafted illusion than a reflection of a genuine affinity between the poet and the politician. But beyond the personal careerist motivations of the letter, of chief significance for the purpose of my larger argument is the fact that it assumes a self-evident connection between classical clarity—the rejection of Asiatic *voluptas*—and performative efficacy. Quevedo's tendentious use of the eulogy to attack *culteranos* is readily evident; he brandishes Fray Luis's clarity as a weapon against those who corrupt Spanish by using needlessly artificial language: "Obscurecer lo claro es borrar, y no escribir, y quien habla lo que otros no entienden primero confiesa que no entiende lo que habla" ("Dedicatoria" 38). Recalling the "invasion" of the Attic by the Asiatic,—"Poco ha que esta inorme y fanfarrona parlería de Asia vino a Atenas"—Quevedo launches into a diatribe against the mixture of styles: "Ni sé qué codicia u qué gloria mueve a los charlatanes de mezclas y a los que escriben taracea de razonar, prosa espuria y voces advenedizas y desconocidas de tal suerte que una cláusula no se entiende con la otra" ("Dedicatoria" 48). The stylistic critique is thus laden with a pungent moral judgment reminiscent of the author's burlesque texts where the kind of linguistic flourishes practiced by the *gongoristas* are also tarnished by accusations of unseemly mixture and foreignness. In particular, Quevedo takes issue with the tendency to deliberately avoid common words by replacing them with ones that are thought to sound more dignified, which, he warns, results in both poor taste and depravity: "Sea ejemplo si en España alguno, por escusar la voz *cabrito,* que es decente y no sucia ni vil ni deshonesta, dijese *cuerno,* que es todo esto junto con ignominia y de mala composición de letras" ("Dedicatoria" 54–55). He also decries the use of metaphors that fuse disparate elements—"no se han de buscar de cosas remotas sino de las propincuas y semejantes" ("Dedicatoria" 43)—thus adopting a position diametrically opposed to Gracián's belief that keeping superior language alive depends on building new unexpected conceits. Inverting the relationship between seductive wit and performative value, Quevedo champions simplicity as the only means to the power of action. Just as Fray Luis "nos dio fácil y docta la filosofía de las virtudes," Olivares, the great statesman, "siempre ha escrito tan fácil nuestra lengua" (Quevedo, "Dedicatoria" 37, 42). Quevedo again couples the questionable association of verbal sobriety and political efficacy with that of masculinity and social acumen: he hails Fray Luis as "el mejor blasón de la habla castellana, con inclinación tan severa a los estudios varoniles" ("Dedicatoria" 37).

Although lending lip service to the Quintilianic principle of balance between didactic clarity and artistic polish, Quevedo, in reality, upholds the *utile* to the exclusion of the *dolce,* as can be surmised from his thoughts on the poem by Vicente Espinel that he cites.

> El varón bueno y de prudente pecho
> los versos duros libremente culpa,
> los que carecen de arte reprehende,
> a los mal adornados con la pluma
> una negra señal los pone encima,
> la demasía de ornamento corta,
> los poco claros manda que se aclaren. (qtd. in "Dedicatoria" 46)

Paying no attention to the verses that denounce lack of artfulness, Quevedo's subsequent comments linger only over the point about clarity, emphasizing it further with a quotation from Aristotle about the coldness of obscure language.

Recurrent throughout Quevedo's writings is an insistence that language serve a rallying function. Deliberately separating *Marco Bruto* from genres that seek to excite some pleasure in the audience, Quevedo is emphatic about its militant objective: "Tú, hija de la verdad vanamente disfamada en los hipócritas, gloriosamente asistida en los santos"—"eterna virtud" being the addressee here—"concede a mis escritos la eficacia para persuadirte; porque, siendo más útiles que elegantes, se empleen en el provecho y no en el deleite" (971). Again, the categorical opposition of utility and enjoyment denotes a drastic reversal of Ciceronian civism.

Where Quevedo's contemporaries had seen the need to revise established Christian and classical notions of virtue to meet the challenges of early modern citizenship, they struggled to find ways of retaining a civilizing mission. Recognizing that the intellectual and ethical stability of a providentialist order had been shaken by the rise of secular pragmatism at one extreme and by spectacular illusionism at the other, they adopted the language of prudence as a conciliating resource to harness power and contain brute force. Diverging from the dialogic facets of prudence, Quevedo proposes a tenacious control of reception. That such control occurs as a performative reality only in fleeting acts that defy pacified coexistence betrays an awareness of the unconducive nature of his demand. The substantive connection between word and deed on which Quevedo has so stalwartly insisted ultimately reveals itself to be purely theatrical.

From Classroom to Forum: The Death of the Orator

Reproducing some of Seneca the Elder's *suasoriae*, the third part of *Marco Bruto* initially situates itself in an academic forum. The *suasoriae* at issue, deliberative formulae for or against a given affirmation, were part of a larger collection of such compositions by outstanding Roman orators. As evident from the particular declamations cited by Quevedo, the participants aim to outdo one another in their ingenious responses to the question of whether Cicero should burn his writings in exchange for his life: the choice given him by Mark Antony. All of the cited speeches take the same side, masterfully making their cases for why he should accept death rather than let his writings perish. Quevedo then adds his own declamations on both sides of the question, bringing the work to a close with a vivid dramatization of Cicero's murder at the hands of the enemy. The last speaker is Cicero himself, who confronts his treacherous assassin and one-time protégé: "Mátame y desmiénteme, pues degollando a quien debes la vida pruebas contra mi defensa que mataste a tu padre. Tú exageras la fuerza de mi elocuencia, pues pudo defender de un parricidio a quien en mí comete otro. Sácame del juicio nefario de la ciudad en que pude defenderte y yo no soy defendido." His fiery words are cut short with a swift blow: "Cortóle Popilio con la garganta la voz. Nada pareció imposible sino degollar a Cicerón quien le oía. Dejó el cuerpo sin las manos y la cabeza, y en el Foro clavó la cabeza entre las dos manos, porque sus obras y sus palabras fuesen espectáculo donde fueron milagro" (Quevedo, *Marco* 991).

What, then, are we to make of this ending? In what sense does it resolve the rhetorical quandaries brought up both in the declamations and in the earlier parts of *Marco Bruto?* What conclusions does it draw about the political agency of the well-performed word? Cicero's death is evidently much more than an allegory of the silencing of eloquence under autocratic rule. It encompasses allied preoccupations immediate to Quevedo's own time: the displacement of Ciceronianism by Senecan poetics, the use and definition of rhetoric in the early modern state, a discomfort with the idea of aesthetics detached from political action, and the concomitant despondence vis-à-vis signs of the irrelevance of persuasive language to executive government. When related to Quevedo's treatise as a whole and to the larger framework of his political program, the inclusion of the declamations, the author's own additions to them, and their incorporation as a preface to the murder of this founding figure of civic speech provide closure, albeit a troubled one, to the vexed question of the proper connection between verbal performance and social action.

Needless to say, this is not a defense of Cicero himself, nor of the Tullian style, especially given Quevedo's antipathy for the stilo fiorito and his identification with Senecan bareness. At the same time, the kind of pointed wit displayed by the practitioners of the suasoriae does not precisely adhere to Quevedo's purported oratorical ideals either. The instances of communicative excellence that Quevedo elsewhere upholds as capturing the public imagination, such as Portia's dying speech or Brutus's fiery writing, are envisioned as spontaneous performances endowed with the aura of substantive emanations. By contrast, the cited declamations are studied exercises, the product of a contrived ingenuity dissociated from the fray of real action. That the confrontation between Mark Antony and Cicero is reduced to a prompt for classroom rhetorical contests indicates a loss of political relevance. But Quevedo reinvigorates this academic duel by inventing new declamations and reframing the hortatory competition in relation to bloody conflict. Whereas the compositions collected by Seneca the Elder were created well after Cicero's death and used the orator as a rhetorical persona, Quevedo resituates them in Cicero's time, bringing the root conflict behind the exercises to life. Yet this is not to be read as a celebration of oratorical triumph because the work culminates in the orator's death. It is, rather, as dramatization of a short-lived performative zeal.

To begin with, Quevedo transcribes the suasoriae verbatim. For instance, Asprenas's articulation "Si quemas tus escritos, pocos años te promete Antonio: todos, si no los quemas, el pueblo romano," is superseded by Argentarius's pointed questions "¿Qué no puede éste que puede dar muerte a Cicerón? ¡Qué! ¿No pude guardarle sino más cruelmente que degollándole? ¿Persuádeste ha de perdonarte quien con tu ingenio se indigna? ¿Tú esperas vida déste, que aún no se ha olvidado de tus palabras?" (Quevedo,

Marco 985, 986). Quevedo then incorporates himself into the duel and argues the contrary position, namely, that Cicero should live rather than save his writings. In this sense, he actually adopts a role that Seneca the Elder deemed was missing in the original exercises: "I know of no-one who declaimed the other side in this *suasoria,* everybody worrying about Cicero's books, no-one about Cicero: though in fact that side is not so bad that Cicero would have been unready to consider it if he had really been faced with these terms" (Seneca, *Suasoriae* 2:605). Creating this imaginary situation, Quevedo counters, "Más importa a Cicerón que le oigan, que no que le lean" (*Marco* 987). He proceeds to revive the orator's voice, proclaiming on his behalf that choosing his life over his writing is the true sign of courage: "Yo, Cicerón, te ruego que no mueras confesando que tuviste miedo de vivir." There is, furthermore, no cause to fear the burning of his writings: "Tú puedes quemar las obras que hicistes; mas las que ellas multiplicaron, haciéndose infinitas de cada una, nadie las puede consumir" (Quevedo, *Marco* 988).

Taking the deliberation a step further, Quevedo reflects that the initial question of whether to burn his writings is not even worthy of response, for the tyrant is in a position to annihilate both his enemy's life and works. Hence the best response that Cicero can give is to refuse to answer the question: silence is what would ultimately endow him with the most communicative power. If Cicero says he wants his life, Quevedo argues, he is authorizing Antony to destroy his works; if he says the opposite, he is authorizing him to take his life. In both cases, he would be conceding to his foe. Therefore, to deprive the tyrant of apparent influence and conserve it for himself, Cicero abstains from responding and confronts his fate. In its spectacular rejection of political negotiation, this act stands as the quintessence of eloquent performance. An exemplary realization of Quevedean virtù, the "espectáculo" of Cicero's death is the decisive incarnation of his "obras y sus palabras," claiming for itself a place in the public imagination. The inscription composed for Cicero's tomb further emphasizes the formidable stature of his words: "Aquí yace Marco Tulio, / a quien Marco Antonio, / que nunca temió a Dios, / temió siempre" (Quevedo, *Marco* 991).

Whereas, at one level, words and deeds are rendered continuous here, it would be simplistic to leave things at that. This is a text that registers deep uncertainties about the role of language in the late *antiguo régimen*. The work ends with silence, the orator's voice literally cut off, which can itself be regarded as a grand rhetorical feat on Quevedo's part. What better way to glorify the orator than to record his dying words, which embrace the violence of political action? As Quevedo puts it, "En las cosas que están en manos de la violencia y en poder de la venganza poderosa y de la enemistad armada, no se ha de pedir su parecer al discurso, sino su resolución a la necesidad" (*Marco* 988).

Considering the way in which modern aesthetics in an era of technical reproducibility remembers the loss of direct auratic transmission, Agamben notes, "The survival of the past in the imponderable instant of aesthetic epiphany is, in the final analysis, the alienation effected by the work of art, and this alienation is in its turn nothing other than the measure of the destruction of its transmissibility, that is, of tradition" (*The Man* 107). By this measure, one could say that the performative vitality of tradition is preserved, albeit in an agonistic sense, because it animates an "instant of aesthetic epiphany," which, in turn, recalls its death. A comparable perception pervades Quevedo's treatises. Latent in their depictions of great eloquence is a consciousness of its transience.

In *La Hora de todos,* this consciousness reaches an untenable extreme. Ephemeral performance loses all transcendence: the human word succumbs to the status of lowly printed matter. Represented as base substance, as inchoate sign, the letter comes to signify the end of the "order of the body." The sense of social and material alienation habitually attached to the late modern condition, it would seem, is already palpable here.

4

VACUOUS PRINT

Metílos en paz, diciendo que yo quería aprender virtud resueltamente. [. . .] Y así, que me pusiesen a la escuela, pues sin leer ni escribir, no se podía hacer nada.

Con lo que vos sabéis de latín y retórica, seréis singular en el arte de verdugo.
—Francisco de Quevedo, *La vida del Buscón llamado Don Pablos*

IN ONE OF THE LAST SCENES of Quevedo's vertiginous political satire *La Hora de todos y la Fortuna con seso,* a Morisco recently expelled from Spain urges his sovereign to promote scholarship and literary achievement.[1] To ensure that their glorious deeds live on in public memory, he presses, his people should follow in the footsteps of Spain, where "hoy viven triunfantes las lenguas griega y latina, y en ellas florecen, a pesar de la muerte, sus hazañas y virtudes y nombres" (Quevedo, *La Hora* 297). But the heathen king is quick to refute the celebrated union of arms and letters:

> De su espada, no de su libro, dicen los reyes que tienen sus dominios; los ejércitos, no las universidades, ganan y defienden; victorias, y no disputas, los hacen grandes y formidables. Las batallas dan reinos y coronas; las letras, grados y borlas. En empezando una república a señalar premios a las letras, se ruega con las dignidades a los ociosos, se honra la astucia, se autoriza la malignidad y se premia la negociación; y es fuerza que dependa el victorioso del graduado, y el valiente del doctor, y la espada de la pluma. [. . .] Luego que Cicerón, Bruto, Hortensio y César introdujeron la parola y las declamaciones, ellos propios la turbaron en sedición, y con las conjuras se dieron muerte unos a otros, y otros a sí mismos; y siempre la república, y los emperadores, y el imperio fueron deshechos y por la ambición de los elegantes aprisionados. [. . .] Dices que hoy, por sus grandes autores, viven los varones grandes que tuvieron, que vive su lengua, ya que murió su

monarquía; [. . .] más valiera que viviera la monarquía muda y sin lengua, que vivir la lengua sin la monarquía. Grecia y Roma quedaron ecos: fórmanse en lo hueco y vacío de su majestad, no voz entera, sino apenas cola de la ausencia de la palabra. (Quevedo, *La Hora* 300–301)

The opposition of "la lengua sin la monarquía" to the by far preferable "monarquía muda y sin lengua" brings to mind the declamations pronounced in *Marco Bruto* in favor of Cicero's life over his works. Articulating a more extreme version of the idea at issue there, that words have value only insofar as they are substantively linked to performance, the Turkish ruler suggests an inverse relationship between language and action. This is the central preoccupation of the *La Hora de todos,* which deserves to be read as a monument to the twin fall of culture and politics. In contrast with Quevedo's treatises, which provide models, however tension ridden, of cultural hegemony, his satire *La Hora de todos* (whose presumed dates of composition, 1633–35, overlap with those of *Marco Bruto* and *Política de Dios,* part II) undermines the very possibility of constructing such meaningful illusions.[2] In accordance with the Gran Turco's prognosis, Spain is reduced to "cola de la ausencia de la palabra," epitomizing the demise of both oral *parole* and written *langue*.

I conclude this study of Quevedo's mythical constructions of leadership with a discussion of this satire because it revealingly complements the theory of communication formulated in his noncomic treatises. Not surprisingly, given its genre, *La Hora de todos* is far more virulent in its defiance of early modernity. Focusing on the absence rather than the construction of cultural and political authority, the satire depicts a world that deviates glaringly from the gripping body-centered interactions between audience and representation championed in Quevedo's sententious treatises. It symbolizes social breakdown as a spectacle of systematic disembodiment and dismemberment: we repeatedly witness bodies being obliterated or reduced to inert aggregates.

The work is a composite allegory about the end of transmissibility or "disenchantment," to employ the term used by Weber to designate the displacement of the mystery and magic of charismatic authority characteristic of traditional societies by the rational functionality of modern institutionalization. Well aware that some would claim the latter phenomenon does not altogether apply in the Spanish context, I shall soon make clear the precise sense in which it is to be understood here. My general contention is that the budding concept of centralized statehood plays a key role in Quevedo's vision of cultural collapse.

Before, however, advancing further with this reading, some general remarks on the form and content of *La Hora de todos* are in order. The nature of satire as immoderate medley—*satura*—is fully realized in this multitiered text, which combines moral dogma with topical political critique, doctrinal attack on the corruption of manners with subversive indictment of established systems of government. Quevedo combines mock epic, burlesque caricature, libel, political pamphlet, moral tract, and political treatise in an encompassing vision of early modern urban life. In this regard, we might see in the work's opening definition of itself as "extravagante reloj que dando una hora sola, no hay cosa que no señale con la mano" (Quevedo, *La Hora* 147), a playful reference to its generic elasticity. Most immediately, though, these words refer to the innumerable characters and contexts that are pilloried. Organized as a great theater of the world with the vulgarized gods looking on as Fortuna pays an earthly visit, the "tratadillo" (Quevedo, *La Hora* 147) lampoons a broad spectrum of social types and institutions, from inept doctors to failed international diplomacy.

The work's framing premise, which purportedly ties together its satirical sketches, is the topos of the upside-down world. This is introduced in the prologue, where the Olympian deities, represented in picaresque guise, have been summoned to hear Jupiter air his complaints about Fortune's arbitrariness. Such are "tus locuras, tus disparates y tus maldades," the king of the gods berates her, that "persuades a la gente mortal que [. . .] no hay dioses, y que el cielo está vacío, y que yo soy un dios de mala muerte. Quéjanse que das a los delictos lo que se debe a los méritos, y los premios de la virtud al pecado; que encaramas en los triubunales a los que habías de subir a la horca, que das las dignidades a los que habías de quitar las orejas, que empobreces y abates a quien debieras enriquecer" (Quevedo, *La Hora* 156–57). Jupiter then decrees that, at the appointed hour, Fortune must use her powers to set the world aright. In the different tableaux that follow and make up the body of the text, Fortuna metes out the fate that people deserve. Each of the first twenty-two vignettes satirizes social types from Spanish urban life.[3] Among these are a doctor, a corrupt minister, a culterano poet, a deceptive matchmaker, vain women, a female swindler, a letrado, and job seekers. The doctor is turned into an executioner; the minister is stripped of the house he stole and left with nothing but a "For Rent" sign; the poet's obscure verses are incinerated; the matchmaker is left bickering with the now phantasmatic lowlife he was attempting to sell off to his client; the women feigning youth have their advanced age publicly revealed; the swindler is diminished to a cardboard death mask; the letrado's angry clients denounce him for his useless litigation; the job seekers are faced with the sight of themselves lined up through the centuries, like a train of ghosts.

With the exception of the intercalated vignettes on the hanged criminals, the cheat, and the alchemist, the last tableaux occur in an international setting, with the Hour catching up with, among others, the Dukes of Muscovy and Florence, the Dutch explorers in Chile, the Gran Turco, the king of England, the Republics of Venice and Genoa, and finally with the congress of nations. Once again, the wicked are punished or denounced. But, in general, these vignettes differ somewhat from those of the social types insofar as they tend to include longer—and more ponderous—moral commentary. For instance, the old man who, upon the arrival of the Hour, wrenches the scissors away from the greedy William of Orange as the prince prepares to cut up the map so as to suit his own interests, launches into a lecture on the dangers of imperial expansion, citing the falls of Assyria, Greece, and Rome as cautionary tales. Fortune's call at the Duke of Muscovy's court is punctuated by a speech on the importance of subjects' genuine loyalty to their ruler. The characters in the Gran Turco tableau mentioned at the start of this chapter hold forth on the long-standing debate about arms and letters. The final vignette on the league of nations similarly includes declamations on a variety of core ethical-political issues, from the usurpation of excessive power by princes, to the relative virtues and vices of republican versus monarchical government, to the rise of the favorite. Such reflections are, in turn, layered with topical innuendo, marking the work's role as political pamphlet. As Jean Bourg, Pierre Dupont, and Pierre Geneste have shown, these tableaux are thick with references to current international tensions, and criticism of other European powers is compounded by a denunciation of the diplomatic and military mishaps of the Olivares regime (98–99). Spain, in other words, is as much under fire as her rivals.

The burlesque humor that dominates the initial tableaux does not disappear in the later ones. Where the earlier vignettes demean specific social figures by showing individual bodies denuded, disintegrated, or reduced to phantasmatic shades, several of the later ones do much the same to entire political systems or nations. Thus we have la Imperial Italia, so diminished by geopolitical losses that she is pictured both as a ragged beggar and as a weightless body somersaulting through the air before the avid eyes of foreign rulers eager to benefit from her decline. Among these, the French king covetously doffs his bishop's miter at the airy nation and, in the process, reveals his baldness, "lo calvino de su cabeza" (Quevedo, *La Hora* 236). Quevedo's use of the word "calvino," a reference to both baldness and

Calvinism, characteristically combines corporeal and ideological caricature in a construction that, in turn, pictures political authority as empty posturing. Similar implications of sterility are brought to the fore in the chapter on the congress of nations, which draws to a close with the entire assembly reduced to utter confusion and despondence. The contentious crowd in its animalistic state is likened to the battle between the frogs and the rats from the Homeric parody the *Batracomiomachia*. Utterly dehumanized, the multitude disperses, each member bemoaning his condition: "Se fueron todos quejosos de lo que cada uno pasaba, y rabiando cada uno por trocar su estado con otro" (Quevedo, *La Hora* 366). Again, as he does in the initial tableaux, Quevedo degrades humanity to a barren and exchangeable condition, further emphasizing this vision in his epilogue, which draws the work to a close with a feast, where the drunken gods confirm the inconsequential nature of the drama they have just witnessed. Reflecting that the world is no better off after Fortuna's hour-long journey, Jupiter asks for things to return to their previous condition, which was, he finally decides, preferable. Calling for individuals to take responsibility for their own fates, rather than blaming Fortuna, he reasons, "Y aquel que recibe y hace culpa para sí lo que para sí toma, se queje de sí propio, y no de la Fortuna que lo da con indiferencia y sin malicia. Y a ella le permitimos que se queje de los hombres que, usando mal de sus prosperidades o trabajos, la disfaman y la maldicen" (Quevedo, *La Hora* 368). Then, as humanity and its ills fade into oblivion, the gods turn their attention to the pleasures of a frenzied Dionysian dance. Thus ends the work, leaving it up to its readers to decide how to confront the interpretive challenges it poses.

Jorge Luis Borges dismissed the exegetical complexities of *La Hora de todos,* explaining the work as being monolithically driven by rhetorical exhibitionism. Given its surfeit of verbal ingenio and extreme caricature, we can well understand his counting it among the works to be remembered as "vivas almácigas de tropos" (*Inquisiciones* 81) and his concomitant inattention to its political meaning. In more ways than one, *La Hora de todos* makes a mockery of its purportedly pithy brevity, its claim to economically tell "everything" being undercut by its wayward facetiousness, which seemingly flaunts its status as a book of nothing.

Other critics have, in contrast, resisted Borges's exclusive emphasis on the satire's verbal playfulness. Some have found its abundant and very precise glosses of political affairs, which would have been readily understood by a contemporary audience, to be a measure of Quevedo's critical engagement with current events (Bourg, Dupont, and Geneste; Riandère La Roche,

"Nota," and "La satire"). In Josette Riandère La Roche's view, *La Hora de todos* questions the political establishment by foregrounding its ideological contradictions ("Nota"). Building further on this, William Clamurro has emphasized the satire's contestatory vein, holding that its inflated comedic elements thinly veil Quevedo's political disenfranchisement ("Empire"). The fact that by the time he wrote *La Hora de todos* Quevedo had completely fallen out of sorts with the count-duke's government is, of course, significant. Focusing above all on the international episodes, Clamurro goes so far as to say that *La Hora de todos* gives "voice to a figure representative of a victim of Spain's (or someone else's) imperialism or other acts of oppression" ("Empire" 106). He is quick to point out that the satire is motivated not by idealistic or progressive political causes, but rather by a purely critical spirit, arising in part from Quevedo's status as a "'marginalized insider'" ("Empire" 106). The work's pugnaciousness would be a measure of Quevedo's trenchant traditionalism and not of any desire for change.

But more directly relevant to my argument are those readings that consider both the stylistic and political preoccupations of the work. In an earlier analysis of *La Hora de todos,* Clamurro comments that Quevedo's incorporation of various forms of discourse "has the effect of foregrounding (probably unintentionally) the whole question of discourse itself as a problem, and specifically as an ideological problem, or what we might call the politics of meaning" (*Language* 40). I would contend that the work quite deliberately reflects on the instability of language. In sum, the social role of language itself is as much at issue as the geopolitical setbacks of Olivares's regime.

Already some time ago, James Iffland pointed us in this direction by discussing the sinuous fluctuations of the work between a defense and an undermining of the status quo ("Apocalypse"). Brought to the fore in his analysis is the fundamental tension found in the text between the dissidence of the political libel and the conservative character of the doctrinal attack on human vices, between its serious questioning of authority and its playful verbal exhibitionism. On the one hand, notes Iffland, even though several tableaux question established social hierarchies by exposing the evils of society and its institutions, by concluding in the end that things were indeed better before Fortuna's attempt to correct what was wrong, Quevedo appears to imply that ultimately the dominant order is good. But this message is far from the conclusive one: the last tableau is, after all, as burlesque as the previous ones. In short, as Iffland well notes, the work is best described as a "'condensation' of [. . .] contradictory urges" that are not resolved ("Apocalypse" 102). Of particular pertinence here is the sense in which the satire's conflictedness is rooted in a despondent view of rhetorical invention. By considering Quevedo's conscious reflection about a perceived crisis of language, we can understand how the aporias with which the satire confronts its readers are thematized within it. In its perplexing fluctuation between orthodoxy and subversion, in its ethical indeterminacy, the work shows itself to be a symptom of the problem on which it reflects metatextually: the decline of eloquence in the emergent modern state.

A close look at Quevedo's treatment of this issue in *La Hora de todos,* while keeping in mind the ongoing preoccupation with the social uses of language throughout his corpus, shows the extent to which the dissociation presumed by Borges between stylistic immoderation and the imparting of serious meaning is really a false problem. It results in part, I would suggest, from the anachronical imposition of late modern *écriture*-centered reading practices that do not think about texts within a performative context but take for granted an individualized and silent relationship with them. Meanwhile, the conceptions of rhetoric—classical and Christian—within which Quevedo operates do not dissociate between stylistic and social import. Language and, by extension, other forms of communication are inherently social instruments. What can be said and what is in fact crucial to the present analysis is that Quevedo views this rhetorical model of interaction as being under threat, hence the aporetic nature of *La Hora de todos.*

Because of its antiheroic and profoundly self-parodying nature, satire is a most useful medium, which is exploited by Quevedo to show that the very act of communicating coherently is imperiled, given the changes in the material conditions and concrete functions of language propelled by the nascent modern state. Dramatizing the loss of magical praesentia, *La Hora de todos* exposes the emptiness of all forms of expression, courtly and bureaucratic, elite and popular, written and oral.

The Fallen Republic of Letters

To the extent that the modern condition is defined as the awareness of a substantive difference between past and present (Calinescu; Poggioli), *La Hora de todos* is strikingly modern in its formulation of the mortality of tradition. If we bear in mind current historiography on antiguo régimen Spain, the alarmism of Quevedo's vision becomes quite patent. "Spain in many respects gave the appearance of being little more than a heterogeneous collection of town units," says Henry Kamen (*Spain* 3), alluding to the continued identification of Spaniards with traditional local loyalties rather than with an overarching concept of centralized nation. He later recalls Spain's relative insularity from European intellectual and scientific currents: "In 1664 [Francis] Willughby had observed that 'in all kinds of good learning the Spaniards are behind the rest of Europe, understanding nothing at all but a little of the old wrangling Philosophy and School-divinity'" (*Spain* 319). Yet Willughby's view is reductive, and there is much in Kamen's own account as well as in those of other distinguished historians that qualifies such simplifications. The notions of centralization, pragmatism, and rational administration are fully operative in Madrid's political culture, although they in no way mean the end of the body-centered order.

As in the rest of Europe, so in Spain both tendencies—modernization and attachment to traditional ritual—coexist: "En lo que se refiere a las formas de comunicación, [. . .] se puede dividir el continente en dos Europas, una primera racionalmente moderna, precapitalista y escritófila, y una segunda feudal y católica, anclada en el oscurantismo de la verbofilia y en el sentimentalismo de la visualización barroca" (Bouza, *Del escribano* 24). Whereas much of the population is illiterate and hence functions wholly in the aural and visual realms, there is a growing literate minority that begins to resemble a modern public sphere, making its presence felt in the emergence of economic societies, *salones,* academies, and the increased circulation of printed matter (López 49–50).[4] A particularly conspicuous sign of the robust existence of public opinion would be the surge, between the reigns of Philip III and Philip IV, in newsletters and current events pamphlets, reporting on everything from substantive political development to court social rumor (Ettinghausen). Within the literate world—as has been amply discussed—reading, seeing, and hearing continue to be thought of as mutually complementary activities. The educational system is still very much centered on rhetoric, visualization being an integral part of memorization and declamation the ultimate objective (Bouza, *Del escribano* 24–25, 52–53). At the same time, though yet far from the muted textual world of late modernity, the conception of writing in Quevedo's era is undergoing change: attributes specific to this medium are gaining public recognition as attested to by a growing number of eulogies of both the written and printed word (Bouza, *Del escribano* 56–57). Such works vindicate writing as an ideal channel for secretive communication, stipulating that it is particularly useful in the political realm and that it can be essential to the king when there are confidential matters at hand (Saavedra Fajardo, *Empresas* 281; Bouza, *Del escribano* 77). In more general terms, the lettered classes value writing as a privileged form of communication, essential to civilized existence and superior to speaking insofar as the spoken word is ephemeral, "volandera," whereas the written word is lasting and thus a crucial foundation of government and cultural memory (Bouza, *Del escribano* 30–31).

Rejecting such assumptions, Quevedo expresses profound skepticism both regarding the literate sphere and the governmental machine to which it is connected. Displayed before us in *La Hora de todos* is a large-scale "disembedding" of arts and letters, which lapse into an atomized and a profane existence. Beyond the differences between the domestic and international vignettes of the "tratadillo," represented throughout is the loss of aura, exemplified in vignettes where communication breaks down into uncontrolled expression.

Framing these instances of rhetorical depredation is the advance of la Hora, whose tyrannical mechanized precision is to be contrasted with the balanced Relox in Antonio de Guevara's *Relox de príncipes*:

> Este *Relox de príncipes* no es de arena, ni es de sol, ni es de horas, ni es de agua, sino es relox de vida, porque los otros reloxes sirven para saber qué hora es de noche y qué hora es de día, mas éste nos enseña cómo nos hemos de ocupar cada hora y cómo hemos de ordenar la vida. El fin de tener reloxes es por ordenar las repúblicas, mas este *Relox de príncipes* enséñanos a mejorar las vidas, porque muy poco aprovecha que estén muy concertados los reloxes y que anden en bandos y dissensiones los vezinos. (30)

Despite the initial distinction that Guevara draws between the mechanical clock and the "life" clock, ultimately he does not deny that the two can complement one another, the former allowing for efficacious coordination that is best used if human wisdom prevails. In much seventeenth-century literature, the clock is treated as a moral memento (a symbolic incarnation of *tempus fugit*), which leads to an enlightened *desengaño* (Heiple 149, 168). Deviating from this consolatory intent, Quevedo's representation underscores the clock's material and temporal dominance. Jupiter, "jefe de relojeros" (Quevedo, *La Hora* 161), cries out the specific hour and minute of the day at which Fortuna must operate. She, in turn, is presented as readying her wheels and cords to perfectly synchronize her actions with the timepiece's measures. The systematic movement of the Hour becomes emblematic of a depraved world ever more remote from the workings of divine providence. Thus any relation between higher knowledge and technical craft is denied, the very presence of the latter annihilating the former. Were we, with Daniel

Heiple, to challenge the idea that "science was not important in Spanish Golden Age thought" (2), *La Hora de todos* would make an interesting entry point for a reflection on how the scientific revolution—habitually studied in the framework of northern Europe—is processed in Spanish letters. It is well beyond the boundaries of this study to contribute to this topic in any substantive sense. My point is to note that Quevedo's burlesque rendition of the wayward clock mechanism ought to be read as part of his larger challenge to the rationalization of the political sphere, a domain in which the figure of the machine has gained acceptance.

Before addressing how Quevedo contests the integration of *techné* in contemporary political vocabulary, let us approach *La Hora de todos* in broader terms, as a distortion of humanist conceptions of organicity. We might briefly consider Juan Luis Vives's "Fábula de homine" as a point of contrast. In this Renaissance tale, the theatrum mundi allegory serves to illustrate the fundamental link between social order and practical ingenuity. On the stage of an amphitheater, the main character, Man, transforms himself into numerous shapes before the admiring Olympian gods. His capacity to assume a whole spectrum of guises—from that of beast to that of king of the gods—earns him the regard of his Olympian spectators and, ultimately, a place among them: "Mostró a los dioses inmortales su naturaleza, hermana carnal de la de ellos; una naturaleza, que oculta bajo el cuerpo y la máscara, lo convertía en un animal tan variado, tan engañoso, tan cambiante, como un pulpo y un camaleón, como lo habían visto en escena" (Vives 158). Artifice is here a metaphor for political being in the Aristotelian sense for it refers to the unique sophistication and adaptability of the human intellect deemed a crucial component of social existence. In this scheme, a mythopoeic worldview is still reconcilable with the pragmatic realities of government and self-government. Practical, mythical, and intellectual forms of knowledge are productively fused together through reference to the unity of the disciplines, which capture human experience in all of its boundless variety: "A través de esas letras se nos ha transmitido y están escritas tantas disciplinas, entre las que se incluye también la misma religión, el culto y conocimiento del padre Júpiter y de los otros dioses hermanos, rasgo único que no se encuentra en ningún otro animal excepto en éste que demuestra la relación que tiene con los dioses" (Vives 160). In the spirit of the apologists of writing, who often harp on the divine origins of the word, Vives ratifies that writing and the subjects transmitted through it are emblematic of a higher human function; they exemplify the ideals of the "citizen of the polis," for whom "to live the 'good life' meant to be free from the demands of mere life" (Kahn and Saccamano 3).

The reverse of Vives's celebration of the unity of different branches of learning in an enlightened sociability, Quevedo's satire shows society to be utterly imprisoned in its material condition, lowered to a subhuman status, a Hobbesian state of brutishness. *La Hora de todos* registers the demise of ideals of intellectual fluidity and seamless social interaction, reflecting its author's inability to reconcile those ideals with the appearance of a modern subject who begins to accommodate to the fact that society is somewhat at odds with private desires. Unlike Montaigne's introspective adaptation to a world in which "public service [. . .] is no longer built upon a shared public view" (Hampton 47), Quevedo reads the expansion of government and social interaction outside a personalized controlled sphere not as an emendation of the social body, but as its complete breakdown. In fact, what McLuhan once said of *King Lear* is applicable to *La Hora de todos*: "*King Lear* is a kind of elaborate case history of people translating themselves out of a world of roles into the new world of jobs. This is a process of stripping and denudation" (14). In other words, the onset of a new order that embraces material interest leads to the decomposition of the dense web of meaningful exchange identified with a traditional world in which relationships are charged with intrinsic familial and filial value. Utterly devoid of the tragic grandeur marking Lear's lamentations on his abject "unkinging," Quevedo's grotesque vision of this process, is, in a sense, more categorical in its emphasis on the radical emptiness of the modern order. Stripping it of any redeeming epistemological or sensorial depth, he reduces contemporary existence to the "demand for mere life" (Kahn and Saccamano 3).

In its polarization between traditional and emergent forms of social organization, Quevedo's posthumanist view bespeaks a frontal attack on the cultural adaptations to empiricism occurring at centers of power. Symptomatic of such adaptations would be the Crown's promotion of the development of practical means to further its administrative needs and political interests: the collection and standardization of personal information, the compiling of statistics, the advancement of natural history in tandem with the cataloguing of medicinal plants in the New World, the writing of "official" histories of Spain involving the establishment of archives to be, in turn, linked to the preparation of calendrical reform, and, finally, the constitution of an intellectual and juridical "Corpus Hispanorum" (Quijada and Bustamente 57; Bouza, *Communication* 34). From this perspective, then, it is roundly justifiable to refer to the development of a centralized state with its correspondent epistemological impacts. The very conception of language is altered: "El viejo principio de la 'lengua compañera del imperio' (es decir, del poder), tal como lo definiera Nebrija o antes que él Valla, se ha transformado ahora en 'la ciencia compañera e instrumento del imperio'" (Quijada and Bustamante 57). Even in as highly theatrical a space as the court, the logic of empirical rationality makes its imprint. As was made clear in previous chapters, the ethos of prudence effectively centers on maintaining an analytic distance between the observing self and society: "The court is, if not the first, then certainly among the most important centers of societal rationalization. Insofar as rationalization brings an increase in discipline and self-control, a renunciation of physical violence, and the increased regulation of libidinal impulses, the rationalization of society and the 'psychologization' of the self go hand in hand" (Cascardi 256–57).

Quevedo is not alone in his skepticism of incipient professionalization. No longer linked to a harmonious *vivere civile,* the exercise of ingenuity in its various forms is, in his era, tainted by its possible Machiavellian association to dissemblance and moral relativism; in addition, the notion of mechanical craft is colored by negative identification to manual work (Heiple 3). As Peter Burke points out, the pragmatic orientation of intellectual competencies involves a renunciation of the concept of universal knowledge and the acceptance of its fragmentation into discrete disciplines (*A Social History* 85). Thus the distinctiveness of Quevedo's work is not that it registers these trends, but that it contests them so relentlessly.

In his *República literaria,* Saavedra Fajardo mocks the dubious uses of various disciplines: rhetoric, mathematics, and law, to name but three. Far more tempered in its criticism than *La Hora de todos,* this "sátira de las ciencias" cautions against the dangers of comic and tragic excess. Distancing himself from Heraclitus, who mourns the limitations of the human condition, and from Democritus, who derides them, the protagonist remarks,

> Yo me reía de ambos, viendo que aquél reñía porque éste no lloraba, y éste se burlaba porque aquél no reía; si bien después me parecieron la una y la otra invidiosas pasiones contra las ciencias, siendo éstas unos atributos o partes principales de Dios, que sin alguna dellas dejaría de serlo. ¿Qué es la poesía sino una llama suya, encendida en pocos; la retórica, una inspiración divina, que nos persuade la virtud; la historia, un espejo suyo de los tiempos pasados, presentes y futuros; la filosofía natural, un esfuerzo de su poder; la moral, una copia de su ser; la astronomía, un ejemplo de su grandeza; la aritmética, una comprehensión de su esencia; la geometría, un instrumento de su govierno en número, peso y medida; la jurisprudencia, un ejercicio

de su justicia, y la medicina, una atención de su benignidad? (Saavedra Fajardo, *República literaria* 144)

Although, in other passages, Saavedra Fajardo signals a cultural demise through repeated allusion to the production of great quantities of paper and worthless books, these phenomena are not shown to obliterate the core essence of the humanities and the sciences, nor do the allegedly bad uses to which they are put diminish their inherent worth. In Quevedo's world, by contrast, they lose all value; moreover, the Aristotelian and Ciceronian notions of political being so important to Baroque political thought are subverted, and the very survival of the *Homo politicus* in the framework of modern statehood is undermined. The notion of "ciencia, compañera de imperio" is viewed as an utter perversion of organic communication. In its fantastical rendition of cultural fragmentation and temporal instability, *La Hora de todos* heralds the schisms linked to the birth of the antithesis of the *Homo politicus,* in Quevedo's eyes, the *Homo typographicus* (McLuhan).

Parodying the State Machine

In his *Leviathan,* Thomas Hobbes conceives of the commonwealth as a vast mechanism, made up of well-differentiated but organically integrated parts:

> Nature (the Art whereby God hath made and governes the World) is by the *Art* of man, as in many other things, so in this also imitated, that it can make an Artificial Animal. For seeing life is but a motion of Limbs, the beginning whereof is in some principall part within; why may we not say, that all *Automata* (Engines that move themselves by springs and wheeles as doth a watch) have an artificiall life? For what is the *Heart,* but a *Spring;* and the *Nerves,* but so many *Strings;* and the *Joynts,* but so many *Wheeles,* giving motion to the whole Body, such as was intended by the Artificer? *Art* goes yet further, imitating that Rationall and most excellent work of Nature, *Man.* For by Art is created that great LEVIATHAN called a COMMON-WEALTH, or STATE, (in latine CIVITAS) which is but an Artificiall Man; though of greater stature and strength than the Naturall, for whose protection and defence it was intended; and in which, the *Soveraignty* is an Artificiall *Soul,* as giving life and motion to the whole body. (9)

Diverging from previous scholars who situated Hobbes within a modern world founded on a contractual—as opposed to a traditional mimetic—relationship between ruling body and subjects, Christopher Pye demonstrates the continued recourse to mythical and affective formulations of power within Hobbesian political theory. In order for subjects to accept the authority of the state, which they themselves have created, it must be impressed upon them that this authority is much superior to them: "The contrived figure of 'Artificial Man' exceeds the power of those who author it. [. . .] Traced to this ambiguous moment where the subject becomes the awed spectator to his own creation, Hobbes's theory of political origins suggests that throughout the Renaissance sovereign power arose out of the exorbitancy of the theatrical itself; for an affective and 'organic' theorist such as Edward Forsett, as well as for Hobbes the proto-modernist, sovereignty is an irreducibly theatrical phenomenon" (Pye 86). This formidable theatrical phenomenon has, of course, a practical purpose: the survival of the citizenry. Without its "artificial" authority, humanity would be in perpetual war: "During the time men live without a common Power to keep them all in awe, they are in that condition which is called Warre; and such a warre, as is of every man, against every man" (Hobbes 88). The logic of self-preservation also informed continental reason-of-state theories. "Men like the jurist Fernando Vázquez de Menchaca [. . .] and the diplomat Diego Saavedra Fajardo could argue, along with [Giovanni] Botero, that although the current shape of the Spanish monarchy may have been determined by dynastic succession, it could now be defended in terms of its capacity to provide security for its members" (Pagden 45). At the same time, like Hobbes, these theorists are deeply wary of reducing the state to a mere survival mechanism: "Simple defense [. . .] could not [. . .] offer sufficient justification for the continuing existence of any state" (Pagden 45). They thus seek a desirable balance between needs and beliefs, in this sense preserving an equilibrium between the pragmatic and ritual functions of government.

In Quevedo's deformed universe, Artificial Man constitutes no improvement upon nature, and the state is a degraded mechanism, defenseless against Fortune, which, far from preventing perpetual war among its citizens, incites it. Following the rhythm of the great timepiece, Fortuna throws the world into the chaos that it merits:

> Y diciendo y haciendo empezó a untar el eje de su rueda y encajar manijas y mudar clavos y enredar cuerdas, aflojar unas y estirar otras, cuando el Sol, dando un grito, dijo: "Las cuatro son, ni más ni menos:

que ahora acabo de dorar la cuarta sombra postmeridiana de las narices de los relojes del Sol."

En diciendo estas palabras, la Fortuna, como quien toca sinfonía, empezó a desatar su rueda, que, arrebatada en huracanes y vueltas, mezcló en nunca vista confusión todas las cosas del mundo. (Quevedo, *La Hora* 161–62)

The inverse of Hobbes's Artificer, as of Guevara's Relox—and no doubt an incarnation of Machiavelli's wayward lady—Fortuna trips around on the wheel that controls her journey, raveling and unraveling the cosmic mechanism with no reasoned intent: "Traía por chapines una bola sobre que venía de puntillas, y hecha pepita de una rueda que la cercaba como centro, encordelada de hilos, trenzas y cintas, cordeles y sogas, que con sus vueltas se tejían y destejían" (Quevedo, *La Hora* 154).

While thinking about how such images parody the pervasive idea of good leadership as a machine, let us recall Saavedra Fajardo's use of the clock as another obvious point of contrast. In his *Empresas políticas,* the clock with the inscription "Vni Reddatvr," meaning "All Is to Be Reduced to One" (fig. 11), connotes a symbiotic relationship between the effective illusion of unified power and the rational coordination of differentiated functions: "Obran en el reloj las ruedas con tan mudo y oculto silencio, que ni se ven ni se oyen. Y aunque dellas pende todo el artificio, no le atribuyen a sí, antes consultan a la mano su movimiento, y ella sola distingue y señala las horas, mostrándose al pueblo autora de sus puntos. Este concierto y correspondencia se ha de hallar entre el príncipe y sus consejeros" (663–64). What we have, then, in *La Hora de todos* is a systematic caricature of such synthesis, the clock being but one of many subverted symbols of a rationalized *monarchia universalis.*

Another such parodied symbol is the spyglass appearing in the encounter of the Dutch explorers with Chilean Indians who question the invaders' intent: "Instrumento que halla mancha en el sol, y averigua mentiras en la luna, y descubre lo que el cielo esconde, es instrumento revoltoso, es chisme de vidrio, y no puede ser bienquisto del cielo. Traer a sí lo que está lejos es sospechoso para los que estamos lejos. [. . .] Con este artificio espulgáis los elementos, metéisos de mogollón a reinar: vosotros vivís enjutos debajo del agua, y sois tramposos del mar. No será nuestra tierra tan boba que quiera por amigos los que son malos para vasallos" (Quevedo, *La Hora* 311–12). The denunciation of the Dutch expedition is manifestly doctrinal in its condemnation of corrupted worldly ambition. Moreover, like the clock,

FIG 11. Emblem, "Vni Reddatvr," in Saavedra Fajardo's *Idea de un principe politico christiano representada en cien empresas,* 1640. Artist unknown. Biblioteca Nacional de España.

the spyglass is a conventional moral icon, commonly used by emblematists, as is also the case with spectacles, to signify the deformation of reality by the passions (Saavedra Fajardo, *Empresas* 242). In Quevedo's text, the spyglass acquires a pointed historical specificity, associated as it is with a dubious colonial enterprise.

For added clarity on the parodic charge of Quevedo's vignette, it is again worth resorting to Saavedra Fajardo's depictions of the imperial state. In particular, we might compare the vignette on the Dutch explorers with the chapter from *Empresas políticas* on the advantages of navigation. The content of the chapter is summed up by the title emblem, which shows two ships holding up the poles of the globe placed between them (fig. 12). Saavedra Fajardo then elaborates on the links between sea power, commerce, and political supremacy and reflects on the importance of promoting them through the propagation of legendary fictions:

> Ingeniosos los griegos, envolvieron en fingidos acontecimientos [. . .] la moral y la política [. . .] por imprimillas mejor en los ánimos con lo dulce y entretenido de las fábulas. Queriendo, pues, significar el poder de la navegación y las riquezas que con ella se adquieren, fingieron haber aquella nave Argos [. . .] conquistado el vellocino, piel de un carnero, que en vez de lana daba oro, cuya hazaña mereció que fuese consagrada a Palas, diosa de las armas, y trasladada al firmamento por una de sus constelaciones en premio de sus peligrosos viajes, habiendo descubierto al mundo que se podían con el remo y con la vela abrir caminos entre los montes de las olas y conducir por ellos al paso del viento las armas y el comercio a todas partes. (*Empresas* 775)

In the same way, he suggests, Spanish colonial power relies upon the conquest of the sea, which is, in turn, stimulated by the dissemination of Christian myth that aligns the enterprise with "el divino pan del Sacramento" and Hebrew prophesy (*Empresas* 780).

In *La Hora de todos,* the productive symbiosis between politics and myth is undone: the sacrality of empire is shown to be but a flimsy fiction. Quevedo reduces the Prince of Orange, for instance, to a cardboard effigy: "Y diciendo y haciendo, echó la tijera a diestro y a siniestro trasquilando costas y golfos, y de las cercenaduras del mundo se fabricó una corona, y se erigió en majestad de cartón" (*La Hora* 260). At a time when the political shortcomings of Philip IV were everyday topics of conversation, this image of the cardboard prince and his make-believe authority would inevitably evoke Spain's own crisis of monarchical legitimacy.

We are, then, in a symbolic terrain symmetrically opposite to that of the protonationalist *España defendida y los tiempos de ahora* (1609), Quevedo's early incursion into humanist historiography, which had sought to create the illusion of a substantive cultural whole. "La nación española imaginada por

FIG 12. Emblem, "His Polis," in Saavedra Fajardo's *Idea de un principe politico christiano representada en cien empresas,* 1640. Artist unknown. Biblioteca Nacional de España.

Quevedo habita el mismo territorio, posee una memoria histórica común, habla la misma lengua, practica unas costumbres semejantes, se identifica en una religión y posee un representante simbólico único" (Vivar 110). There Quevedo foregrounds cultural and regional particularities, holding forth on the fertility of Spain's soil, the origins of its population, the early Latin, Greek, and Hebrew influences on the Spanish language, and its subsequent development. At the same time, he assigns Spain a universal importance, noting that her greatest problem is that she does not have the renown that she deserves. Antithetical to the disregard for the cultivation of letters voiced by the Gran Turco, the prologue to *España defendida* proclaims, "Ya, pues, es razón que despertemos y logremos parte del ocio que alcanzamos en mostrar lo que es España y lo que ha sido siempre, y juntamente que nunca tan gloriosa triunfó de letras y armas como hoy, gobernada por Don Philipe III, nuestro señor. Tenemos dos cosas que llorar los españoles: la una lo que de nuestras cosas no se ha escrito, y lo otro que hasta ahora lo que se ha escrito ha sido tan malo, que viven contentas con su olvido las cosas a que no se han atrevido nuestros cronistas" (551). By this measure, the existence of Spain is dependent on the construction of a cultural memory in which letters play a key role. To secure universal validity, her present political apogee needs to be connected to an immortalized past, an enterprise in which Quevedo inscribes his own work.

In *La Hora de todos*, Quevedo dissolves the notion of a universalized cultural particularity into a phantasmagoric global pantomime. In the past, the term "phantasmagoric" has been applied to Quevedo's grotesque caricatures and has been read as part of a doctrinal discourse on the vanity of the mortal condition (Iffland, *Quevedo* 77; Lida 235). The dehumanized vacuous bodies of Quevedo's *Los sueños* can, from this perspective, be viewed as iconic representations of human *vanitas*. But, in *La Hora de todos*, the use of the "tempus fugit" topos transgresses the parameters of orthodox moral lesson, attributing a cadaveral nature not only to individuals and specific instances of systemic corruption, but also to Spain as a whole. In portraying the mythical projections of the Habsburg state as vapid fancies, Quevedo undercuts the very foundations of social cohesion.

Figures like the blind and insolent Fortuna and her bald handmaid, Ocasión, Mars clanging pots and pans, or Jupiter turned picaresque "Coime" can be read as travesties of celebratory representations of omnipotent monarchical authority, such as those described by Francisco Pacheco: "Y así la ciega gentilidad, queriendo celebrar a Júpiter, Minerva, Neptuno y otros, ningún camino halló mejor que fabricarles estatuas, y simulacros en grande número. [. . .] Y así no es maravilla que la ley cristiana, valiéndose del mismo medio (pero con fin divino y sacrosanto) haya admitido el uso de las sagradas imágenes, para honrar al verdadero Dios en sus santos y, con este medio, estender más su infinito poder, misericordia, justicia y sabiduría, y difundir por todos los confines de la tierra la gloria y majestad de su nombre" (*El arte* 250). The identification of the Catholic monarchy with the classical deities hence played a key role in the symbolic fusion of ethical principle, efficacious government, and natural order, well exemplified in emblems such as Mendo's bearing the motto "Consvlendvm in Ardvis," that is, "Seek Advice in Difficult Situations," illustrated through the figure of Jupiter, wearing a crown and bearing scepter and lightning bolts, with his counsel of twelve gods. Just as the pagan king of the gods consulted with his aides before punishing the mortals with lightning bolts, so the subscript reads, "En nuestra España siempre se han valido sus Monarchas del consejo de Ministros grandes. [. . .] Oygalos el Príncipe, y execute, como acciones propias, las que después de bien pesadas en las balanzas de la razón, parecieren más ajustadas" (Bernat Vistarini, Cull, and Vodoklys 453). Another telling mark of the embeddedness of Tridentine symbolism in Graeco-Roman myth is the pervasive use of the eagle—one of the forms that Jupiter took—as a royal icon. An emblem by Francisco Núñez de Cepeda shows an eagle on a pedestal bearing a chalice in one claw and a bundle of lightning bolts in the other. "Spicula Differt," that is, "Deflect the Arrows," reads the banderole. The accompanying commentary explains that, as the pagan deity tempered his lightning bolts by offering nectar, so "en el Príncipe Eclesiástico, ha de ser prompta la beneficencia, y tarda la vengança" (Bernat Vistarini, Cull, and Vodoklys 46).

Central to the display of political right, classical images are also, Pacheco states, fundamental to the exhibition of political might and to the justification of dominion (*El arte*). Perhaps best known among these is the motto "Plus ultra," originally adopted by Charles V. It was habitually accompanied by two columns, references to Hercules' marking of the end of the known world, beyond which a glorious Spain would venture. Similarly cosmic in its projection is the hieroglyph included in Pedro Rodríguez de Monforte's "*Descripcion*" of the funerary honors for Philip IV's death (fig. 13), itself symbolized as a sun partly shrouded by clouds. Counteracting the unsettling idea of the king's bodily demise through analogy with the sun's eternal movement, the artist displays two additional suns shining below, signaling the continuity of the dynasty in its heirs. The planetary magnitude of Catholic kingship is also exhibited in Juan de Noort's bust of Philip IV, flanked by Religion and Faith, symbolized by female figures who hold a crown above the king's head, which is itself topped by a sun (fig. 14). Both Faith, who is blindfolded—just as is often the case with Fortuna, arguably her pagan opposite—and Religion have one foot on a globe, thereby signaling the inscription of Spanish dynastic rule in a universal and providential scheme.

FIG 13. Emblem, "Impeditvs Est Sol, et Vna Dies Facta Est, qvasi Dvo," in Rodríguez de Monforte's *Descripcion de las honras que se hicieron a la catholica Magestad de D. Phelippe quarto*, 1666. Artist unknown. Biblioteca Nacional de España.

FIG 14. Juan de Noort, *Philip IV Flanked by Religion* (left) *and Faith* (right), in Láinez's *El privado christiano*, 1641. Biblioteca Nacional de España.

Reflecting upon the intertwining of particular historical events and classical mythical figurations in Cervantes's *La Numancia,* Frederick de Armas points out the ordering function of such imaginative fusions: "Analogical thinking imparts a cohesive and compelling meaning to random historical events. Through an elemental play that views the cosmos in terms of a particular siege, *La Numancia* claims a greater authority than history since the play, as [Carlos] Fuentes has argued, 'descubre la relación existente entre todas las cosas y las religa entre sí'" (*Cervantes* 181). By contrast, the epistemological objective in *La Hora de todos* is to undo such ordering linkages, to accentuate the randomness of mortal life, or, to use the term employed by Jacques Lezra, its "eventiality," that is, its status as an accidental phenomenon, still overrun by primeval pulsions resistant to the stabilizing patterns of historical myth (162).

Quevedo's satire, then, subverts the paradigmatic organicity of historical imperial symbols, dislodging them from the providential and natural teleologies that give them stable meaning. Thus deracinated, the state machine is reduced to a delusion. The critical magnitude of this parody cannot be underestimated; indeed, the argument typically made by traditional satirists, that their work served socially constructive purposes (Spacks 360), does not hold where *La Hora de todos* is concerned. Whereas, in his *The Praise of Folly,* Erasmus claimed that his mockery of corrupted clergymen was an attack on deviant individuals and not on the Church (150–51), Quevedo's satire calls into question the institutional and conceptual foundations of his society.

In this respect also, *La Hora de todos* goes well beyond the bounds of mere political libel. Not stopping at global monarchy, Quevedo ridicules all forms of rule and hence the very notion of human governability itself. He describes republics and monarchies, empires and small fiefdoms as disintegrating, ravaged by mismanagement and greed, their remains finally devoured by their neighbors: "La Imperial Italia, a quien sólo quedó lo augusto del nombre, viendo gastada su monarquía en pedazos, con que añadieron tan diferentes príncipes sus dominios, y ocupada su jurisdición en remendar señoríos, poco antes desarrapados; [. . .] hallándose pobre y sumamente ligera, por haber dejado el peso de tantas provincias, dio en volantín" (*La Hora* 234). All political forms are equally eroded. The subjects of princes are as disgruntled as the citizens of republics, as is made clear in the last tableau of Fortuna's visit, a fictional rendition of the international congress called by the pope to resolve litigious tensions, an encounter that, at Olivares's request, was to take place at Liege (Quevedo, *La Hora* 346n602). Rampant dissatisfaction prevails over the possibility of mending what has gone askew: "Los republicanos querían príncipes, los vasallos de los príncipes querían ser republicanos" (Quevedo,

La Hora 347). In the course of the assembly, a noble Saboyan complains bitterly of being trapped in endless cycles of war in which his duke, incited by both France and Spain, chooses to engage. In response, another speaker launches into a defense of monarchy, arguing that it is better to be directed by one head than by many:

> Si mandan por igual nobles y plebeyos, es una junta de perros y gatos, que los unos proponen mordiscones con los dientes, ladrando, y los otros responden con los araños y las uñas. Si es de pobres y ricos desprecian a los pobres, los pobres envidian a los ricos: mirad qué compuesto resultará de envidia y desprecio. Si el gobierno está en los plebeyos, ni los querrán sufrir los nobles, ni ellos podrán sufrir el no serlo. Pues si los nobles sólo mandan, no hallo otra comparación a los súbditos sino la de los condenados, y éstos somos los plebeyos ginoveses. [. . .] ¿No conoces que nobles y plebeyos transfieren su poder en los reyes y príncipes, donde, apartado de la soberanía de los unos y de la humildad de los otros, compone una cabeza asistida de pacífica y desinteresada majestad, en quien ni la nobleza presume ni la plebe padece? (Quevedo, *La Hora* 350–51)

The dialogue ends in unbridled antagonism. Moreover, the traditional image evoked here of the monarch as the guiding head of the political body cannot be taken seriously. Through figures like the make-believe cardboard king and Jupiter rendered fickle picaresque spectator—an obvious caricature of the mighty Olympian as a panegyrical symbol for the Habsburg sovereign—monarchy is also discredited. We are confronted with a "post-theatrical" universe in which the representational power of "hypostasized" authority is undercut (Pye 86).

The Body Commodified

At the start of his *Restauración política de España* (1619), Sancho de Moncada makes an assertion with which most early moderns would have concurred:

> A muchos parece eterna la Monarquía de España por su grandeza. Pero mucho se habla de su peligro en todas partes, y estos días se ha advertido a V. Majestad en varios libros, y memoriales. Y aunque algunos fundan su temor en parecerles que fueron avisos los de la

> campana de Velilla, y otros en un cometa que estos días han visto, dejadas estas cosas, parece ser de consideración las que he visto en algunos ponderadas. [. . .] Con tales causas no hay prometerse seguridad, pues las Monarquías son tan mortales como los hombres, que es la Monarquía muchos hombres y todos mortales. (96–97)

Departing from the premise that the Spanish monarchy is mortal because it is made up of mortals, Moncada proposes tactical remedies for its malaise. In keeping with this pragmatic discourse, he characterizes the ruler as "médico [. . .] de esta república" (96–97), thereby highlighting the technical aspects of his work. Because Spain's ills are the results not of human vice but rather of faulty judgment, they can be remedied through strategic policies. It is shown that the current crisis is precipitated by local problems, such as the relative paucity of domestically produced goods, a declining population and, more generally, a mismanagement of the colonial enterprise that has resulted in uncontrolled inflation. Among the solutions suggested is that the *vellón*—the copper coin largely responsible for the economic crisis of the seventeenth century—be adjusted in its size and weight to reflect the worth of the metal in it.

From the standpoint of the larger public, such material pragmatism is still rather avant-garde for its time, as evidenced by the common ridiculing of the *arbitrista* in literary works (Vilar Berrogain). Nevertheless, in the governmental sphere, even though arbitristas were somewhat controversial because of the sometimes preposterous nature of their recipes for financial reform (Álamos de Barrientos, *Discurso* 121), a number of their policies made good sense (Elliott, *Imperial Spain* 300). More significant, the principle that judicious economic management was crucial to public well-being was widely accepted among the political elite. As Álamos de Barrientos says in his 1598 *Discurso político al rey Felipe III,* a series of practical recommendations addressed to the king at the start of his reign, "Lo que más conserva la fe del pueblo y la sustenta en obediencia gustosa y sosegada, es ver la riqueza de su rey y el fruto de sus tributos no gastados sin provecho, sino guardados para las necesidades públicas y forzosas" (120). This is reaffirmed even in more theoretical pieces. Mirrors of princes sometimes include financial considerations along with their ethical and political programs. In his *Teatro monárquico de España,* Portocarrero y Guzmán remarks that the "hacienda y caudal es el nervio de la monarquía; es la sangre de aquel cuerpo que lo alimenta y da fuerzas para poder con vigor y robustez, sobrellevar las enfermedades que suele padecer" (169), an assertion also corroborated by Saavedra Fajardo's *Empresas políticas* (775–76).

Given Quevedo's ideological recalcitrance, the intense aversion to commercialization in *La Hora de todos* comes as no surprise. But what is worth detailed attention is that the satire does not limit itself to an attack on arbitristas or other greedy businessmen but imagines a universal contamination of all human interaction by economic exchange. In its portrayals of money lenders and usurers who charge exorbitant interest, requiring that vellón loans be paid back in silver, *La Hora de todos* makes precise references to Spain's dire financial predicament (chs. 5 and 16), formulating it as a grand narrative of human fickleness: "La Moneda es la Circe que todo lo que se le llega o de ella se enamora lo muda en varias formas" (342). Indeed, the counterfeit logic of the arbitristas' policies spreads to all instances of social rapport. Just as the nonsensical policy makers propose, "'Arbitrio fácil y gustoso y justificado, para tener gran suma de millones, en que los que los han de pagar no lo han de sentir, antes han de entender que se los dan'" (Quevedo, *La Hora* 202), so the rest of society presents itself as what it is not. The old woman disguises her true condition as "calavera confitada en untos" with layers of makeup; the matchmaker uses his wit to portray his client's worthlessness as worth: "Señor, la nobleza, no digo nada, porque, gloria a Dios, a v.m. le sobra para prestar; hacienda, v.m. no la ha menester; hermosura, en las mujeres proprias, antes se debe huir por peligro; entendimiento, v.m. la ha de gobernar, y no la quiere para letrado; condición, no la tiene; los años que tiene son pocos—y decía entre sí 'por vivir'—; lo demás es a pedir de boca." (Quevedo, *La Hora* 182, 173). Says Quevedo of his patchwork of lies, "Hurta y miente y engaña y remienda y añade." When the Hour arrives, the matchmaker "se halló desposado con la fantasma que pretendía pegar al otro, y hundiéndose a voces sobre '¿quién sois vos?,' '¿qué trujisteis vos?' 'no merecéis descalzarme,' se fueron comiendo a bocados" (*La Hora* 174). Departing from the Hobbesian notion that the desire for self-preservation or (pace Bentham) for pleasure can motivate individuals to maintain communal order, Quevedo focuses on how the forces of self-interest lead to the demise of the civilized coexistence. The *zoon politikon* degenerates into pure animality. Broken down, in other words, is the division "between the *animalitas* and the *humanitas* of man" on which, Agamben reminds us, the polis was founded (*The Open* 75).

Quevedo's repeated allusions to worldly vanitas might prompt us to explain away his antimercantilist stance as simply a doctrinal traditionalism. Indeed, the world of endless vying for limited resources is the reverse of the sacramental order depicted in *Política de Dios,* in which the irreducible presence of the monarchical body is an inexhaustible source of public nourishment.

In the realm of Christian devotion, the perfidy of interested calculation is eliminated. Giving and receiving are laden with transcendental connotations: whether through God's grace or the human being's giving of himself to divine will, both giver and receiver are substantively bound together in a mutually enriching experience. Vested as he is in this vision, Quevedo cannot but regard the realities of his world as a perversion of eucharistic communion. I would add that, far more than a reflection on mortal fallibility, operative here is a radical skepticism: recalcitrant orthodoxy has evolved into the undermining of tradition. In its dooming association of expanding state machine and disintegrating body politic, *La Hora de todos* anticipates late modern concerns about massification and commodification as the end of social and cultural organicity. We are reminded of José Ortega y Gasset's ominous description of a volatile world in which all public spaces are filled to excess by the unthinking appetitive technocratic masses (37–38, 49).

In the course of la Hora's advance, we are confronted with a dizzying panorama of city life, of social and professional types that extreme caricature renders indistinct from one another, many literally presented as part of a crowd. Among the most evident examples would be the tableau in which thirty-two candidates vie for a position: "Mostraban los semblantes aciagos, y las coyunturas azogadas de reverencias y sumisiones; a cada movimiento de la puerta, se estremecían de acatamientos, bamboleándose con alferecía solícita; tenían ajadas las caras con la frecuencia de gestos meritorios, flechados de obediencia, con las espaldas en jiba" (Quevedo, *La Hora* 221–22). Distraught by such an onslaught, the employer says that he wants to give the job to one but to make everyone happy. With the arrival of the Hour,

> el señor los dejó sobreviviéndose y trasmatándose unos a otros, y se fue podrido de ver que se arrempujaban las edades hacia el *saeculum per ignem*. [. . .] El que pescó el oficio estaba atónito viéndose con tan larga retahíla de herederos; fuese tomándose el pulso, y proponiendo de no cenar, y de guardarse de soles. Los demás se miraban como venenos eslabonados, y, anatematizándose las vidas, se iban levantando achaques y añadiéndose años, y amenazándose de ataúdes, y zahiriéndose la buena disposición, y enfermándose la salud de sus precedentes, y dándose a médicos como a perros. (Quevedo, *La Hora* 225)

In reaction to the struggle among vying candidates, the alarmed gentleman reflects that "el tener qué dar era la mejor cosa del mundo si no hubiera quien lo pretendiera, y que las mercedes, para no ser persecución del que las hace, habían de ser recibidas y no solicitadas" (Quevedo, *La Hora* 223). Thus the gentleman's feudal conception of godlike concession is displaced by a contractual system based on competition for limited goods.

It could be argued that there is a generalized sense of epistemological crisis in peer political writers of the period—for example, Saavedra Fajardo and Gracián—whose renunciation of universal moral absolutes in favor of a prudent realism is marked by a strong skepticism concerning the power of human perception (Robbins 88, 91, 108, 225). And yet, beyond their doctrinal and philosophical doubts about the limitations of worldly knowledge, those writers prefigure the empirical spirit of the Enlightenment in their recognition that a reasoned pragmatism, whatever its limitations, is the only effective means to preserve order (Robbins 230). By contrast, in *La Hora de todos,* Quevedo categorically negates consequential human action; here epistemological crisis takes a nihilistic turn. Far from approaching Enlightenment mentalities, the work's subversive opposition between genuine communication and the material development of the early modern state evokes a despondence characteristic of twentieth-century visions that fear the end of meaningful life in mechanized societies. In its denial of the continued social significance of extant cultural practices, in the trenchancy of its antihumanist stance, Quevedo's satire conceives of historical change as a teleological scheme gone awry.

In this story about the demise of tradition, the rise of print plays a key role. Brought to mind here is McLuhan's controversial definition of "typographic man" as signifying the end of an organic integration of the senses. Reflecting on the remove of the printed word from live speech, McLuhan states that "balanced interplay of the senses became extremely difficult after print stepped up the visual component in Western experience to extreme intensity" (28). Similarly, Quevedo characterizes printed matter as the nemesis of a naturalized *praesentia*. As will be contended in the following pages, the linguistic disintegration that mirrors the decomposition of the body politic is linked to the "alienated" condition of the printed letter.

Typographic Man

We recall that in his letter on Fray Luis de León's poetry, Quevedo attacks Gongorism for its "unmanly" foreignness and lack of stylistic cohesion. Indeed, he makes repeated mention of the tattered and bastardized condition of the Spanish language throughout his writings. In "Cuento de cuentos," we read,

> La habla que llamamos castellana y romance, tiene por dueños a todas las naciones: los árabes, los hebreos, los griegos y los romanos naturalizaron con la vitoria tantas veces nuestro idioma, que le sucede lo que a la capa del pobre, que son tantos los remiendos, que su paño se equivoca con ellos.
>
> También se ha hecho *Tesoro de la lengua española,* donde el papel es más que la razón, obra grande y erudición desaliñada. Ninguno ha escrito gramática, y hablamos la costumbre y no la verdad, con solecismos. (Quevedo, *Prosa* 389)

Nor does Quevedo reserve such attributions of illegitimacy solely for cultivated language. Popular speech also comes under assault: "*Mire lo que le digo* decimos todos por *óigame,* pues no se parecen los [ojos] a las orejas. [. . .] *Aqueste* por este: *agora* por *ahora*; son infinitas las veces en que pudiendo escoger usamos lo peor" (Quevedo, *Prosa* 390). "Considere vuesa merced," he goes on to say, "el buen talle destas voces, que se nos hacen reacias en la lengua y no las podemos escupir: *zurriburri, a cada trique traque, traque barraque, zis zas, zipe zape, abarrisco, irse achito, chitón, con sus once de oveja, troche moche, cochite hervite*; es decir, que no tienen vergüenza para deslizarse en una historia y entremeterse en un sermón, y están ya tan halladas que pocas plumas las desdeñan" (*Prosa* 392–93). Given the mixed repertoire of usages that nourishes his own writings, the blatant irony of this accusation is evident.

Thus, too, in the international congress of *La Hora de todos,* where the Hour completes its course, dialogue decays to noise: "Calló, y como era multitud diferente en naciones y lenguas, se armó un zurrido de jerigonzas tan confuso, que parecía haberse apeado allí la tabaola de la torre de Nembrot: ni los entendían ni se entendían. Ardíase en sedición y discordia el sitio y en los visajes y acciones parecía junta de locos o endemoniados" (364). No longer the pillar of empire once celebrated by Nebrija nor a vehicle of active social fashioning, language has become a sterile mechanism. All verbal expression, written and oral, cultivated and popular, professional and colloquial is portrayed as vacuous exchange. Like the matchmaker who spews words with no outside grounding (Quevedo, *La Hora* 173), the languages of the *poeta culto,* the *hablador plenario,* and the letrado are empty. It is worth looking at some of the particulars to observe Quevedo's repeated exploitation of the same motifs: "Un hablador plenario, que de lo que le sobra de palabras a dos leguas pueden moler otros diez habladores, estaba anegando en prosa su barrio, desatada la tarabilla en diluvios de conversación. Cogióle la HORA, y quedó tartamudo y tan zancajoso de pronunciación, que, a cada letra que pronunciaba, se ahorcaba en pujos de *b-a ba*; y como el pobre padecía, paró la lluvia con la retención, y empezó a rebosar charla por los ojos y por los oídos" (*La Hora* 170). Similarly, the cultista poet is caught "leyendo una canción cultísima, tan atestada de latines y tapida de jerigonzas, tan zabucada de cláusulas y cortada de paréntesis, que el auditorio pudiera comulgar de puro en ayunas que estaba" (Quevedo, *La Hora* 174–75). We should note that here Quevedo expresses the fragmentation of language through its division into parentheses and clauses, forms identifiable with the written and printed word.

A similar idea surfaces in his portrayal of the lawyer who serves as a parody of the classical orator and who, we are told, has gained great fame because of his resounding voice, the efficaciousness of his gestures, and the torrent of words in which he entangles other lawyers. "Y con esto," writes Quevedo, "a unos ordenaba peticiones, a otros querellas, a otros interrogatorios, a otros protestas, a otros súplicas, a otros requerimientos. Andaban al retortero los Bártulos, los Baldos, los Abades, los Surdos, los Farinacios, los Tuscos, los Cujacios, los Fabros, los Ancarranos, el señor presidente Covarrubias, Casaneo, Oldrado, Mascardo, y tras la Ley del Reino, Montalvo y Gregorio López, borrajeados de párrafos con dos corcovas, de la *ce* abreviatura, y de la *efe* preñada con grande prole de números y su *ibi* a las ancas" (*La Hora* 214–16). Quevedo mocks the tradition of the great jurists listed here as the ultimate perversion of inspired eloquence. He derides the audacious lawyer's words as nothing but stagnant bureaucratic formulae, a conjunction of murky marks on the page. The classical ideal of rhetorical abundance or "coloring" is displaced by a stale mechanical logic, again, the antithesis of sensorial plenitude.

Whereas, in an organic semiotic process, verbal communication is pregnant with the illusion of physical enactment, in the unharnessed semiosis of Quevedo's randomly operated universe, parole and langue are revealed as empty forms, the audience being left "en ayunas." An effacement of the Thomistic book of nature, such hollowed verbiage is a nightmarish version of the sensorial abstraction, or, in other words, the loss of synesthetic expression that McLuhan deems symptomatic of the "cool visual detachment" (28) of print.

In direct opposition to Derrida, who sees depersonalized textual circulation as liberating meaning from the authoritarian control of communication systems based on the notion of presence, Quevedo reads the large-scale circulation and appropriation of linguistic practices beyond the contained reception of a ritual context as a tyrannical corruption of true rhetoric. Whereas, for many early modern letrados, the written word is still infused with the life of the spoken word, for Quevedo in *La Hora de todos,* the spoken word becomes permeated with the presumed lifelessness of the mechanically reproduced word. His satire is a deliberate reaction against the commendation of writing and print as technologies vital to government authority.

The Gran Turco directly attributes the demise of the heroic republican legacy to the establishment of print: "Empero luego se inventó la emprenta contra la artillería, plomo contra plomo, tinta contra pólvora, cañones contra cañones. [. . .] ¿Quién duda que falta el plomo para balas, después que se gasta en moldes fundiendo letras, y el metal en láminas?" (Quevedo, *La Hora* 302–3). We might contrast this image with the more conciliatory treatment of the subject in Saavedra Fajardo's *Empresas,* where the emblem of a press reads, "Ex Fvmo in Lvcem" (fig. 15), that is, "Out of the Smoke into the Light," reflecting that words must pass through the dark messiness of the printing process to reach the light of public recognition.

In *La Hora de todos,* the spreading of culture nurtured by print is viewed as an effacement of genuine social worth: "En dándose una nación a doctos y escritores, el ganso pelado vale más que los mosquetes y lanzas, y la tinta escrita, que la sangre vertida; y al pliego de papel firmado no le resiste el peto fuerte, que se burla de las cóleras del fuego; y una mano cobarde, por un cañón tajado, se sorbe desde el tintero las honras, las rentas, los títulos y las grandezas; mucha gente baja se ha vestido de negro en los tinteros" (300). A literate professionalized public is the ultimate mirror of a fragmented political body: "Dividiérase todo el imperio en confusion de actores, y reos, y jueces, y sobre jueces, y contra jueces; y, en la ocupación de abogados, pasantes, escribientes, relatores, procuradores, solicitadores, secretarios, escribanos, oficiales y alguaciles, se agotaran las gentes; y la guerra, que hoy escoge personas, será forzada a servirse de los inútiles y desechados del ocio contencioso; habrá más pleitos, no porque habrá más razón, sino porque habrá más leyes" (Quevedo, *La Hora* 303). Such perceived splintering of the social and cultural spheres impedes meaningful cohesion or, in Benjaminean terms, eliminates the "aura" of genuine transmission:

FIG 15. Emblem, "Ex Fvmo in Lvcem," in Saavedra Fajardo's *Idea de un principe politico christiano representada en cien empresas,* 1640. Artist unknown. Biblioteca Nacional de España.

Even the most perfect reproduction of a work of art is lacking in one element: its presence in time and space, its unique existence at the place where it happens to be.

[. . .]

The uniqueness of a work of art is inseparable from its being imbedded in the fabric of tradition. This tradition itself is thoroughly alive and extremely changeable. An ancient statue of Venus, for example, stood in a different traditional context with the Greeks, who made it an object of veneration, than with the clerics of the Middle Ages, who viewed it as an ominous idol. Both of them, however, were equally confronted with its uniqueness, that is, its aura. Originally the contextual integration of art in tradition found its expression in the cult. ("The Work" 220–23)

As demonstrated by the aforementioned tableaux of atomized crowds and torrents of senseless speech, the loss of experiential "uniqueness" is of salient concern in *La Hora de todos*. With Benjamin's formulation in mind, we can say that Quevedo reads current cultural practices as a chaotic process of decontextualization in which linguistic formulae are replicated haphazardly. Dissociated from any meaningful mise-en-scène, they burgeon into an anarchic Babel. The act of representation is depleted, reduced to a lifeless copy: "Osan decir que el privado total introduce en el rey, como la muerte en el hombre, *novam formam cadaveris,* nueva forma de cadáver, a que se sigue corrupción y gusanos; arte conforme a la opinión de Aristóteles: en el príncipe *fit resolutio usque ad materiam primam,* quiere decir, no queda alguna cosa de lo que fue, sino la representación" (Quevedo, *La Hora* 361). Far from the promise of a transcendental continuation of being, of Gadamerian "parousia," representation is a pale remnant, remote from what was.

Arguing that Cervantes's *Don Quijote* reflects a perceived lack of coincidence between living and constructed event, Lezra has recently read the work as countering a humanist belief in individual agency. From this perspective, the novel severely destabilizes the subject by representing a radical splintering of material reality, aesthetic representation, narrative intention, and reader reception: "It becomes much harder to dissociate the stories told in *Don Quixote* about the act of naming from disturbing allegories about the contingency of that act, its irrationality, its mechanical, nonsubjective, perhaps even its evential status" (Lezra 156). Similarly, in *La Hora de todos,* language is the product of the alienation of both individual and collective will. No longer having power over a material reality that resists mythical ordering, the word loses referential stability and simply replicates the randomness of a lapsed world.

The Demise of Allegorical Function

The scene on the congress of nations provides a fitting culmination to Quevedo's despondent view of language. In the course of the grand meeting, the discord between nations reaches Babelic proportions: "En esto, los cogió la HORA, y, enfurecidos, unos decían: 'Lobos queremos'; otros: 'Todos son lobos'; otros: 'Todo es uno'; otros: 'Todo es malo'" (Quevedo, *La Hora* 365–66). The only consensus to be reached is that "all is bad," and with that, the crowd eventually disperses. Is this not the message implicit in *La Hora de todos,* which displays a series of spectacles of social disintegration and then comes to a close without any constructive suggestion?

The satire's epilogue, where the gods turn away from the chaotic earthly spectacle to their own revelries, would serve as a crowning confirmation of its vanity. In contrast with the habitual use of *mise-en-abîme* toward a constructive aesthetic and ethical self-awareness—Calderón's *La vida es sueño* would be a well-known example of this—here the play within the play does not serve as a conceptually stabilizing venue. Rather, it reemphasizes the prevalent sense of disorder: no revelation is yielded from the interaction between human actors and divine onlookers. An evident cue for the readers—an allusion to the insignificance of their own perusal of the "tratadillo"—is the fact that, unilluminated by the human play, the deities go on to another equally fatuous entertainment. The earthly drama is left without gods, without a bonding authority, floating in an aimlessly configured cosmos that finds a precursor in Lucretius's theories about the world as a by-product of the indeterminate collision of atoms (Lezra 3). The accusation that "no hay dioses," which so irked Jupiter at the start of the work, is, in the end, not off the mark.

In one of the only instances of enlightened performance to be found in *La Hora de todos,* a letrado present at the congress of nations proposes what can be read as a counterargument to the Gran Turco's denial of a productive link between arms and letters. He evokes an idealized world, where culture and politics, representation and practice operate in humanistic equilibrium: "Los juegos públicos se ordenarán del ejercicio de las armas de fuego y del manejo de todas armas, conforme a la disposición de las batallas, porque sean juntamente de utilidad y entretenimiento, juntamente fiestas y estudios; y entonces será decente frecuentar los teatros cuando fueren academias" (Quevedo, *La Hora* 359–60). In this harmonious world, the functional citizen can flourish: "La pretensión que todos tenemos es la libertad de todos, procurando que nuestra sujeción sea a lo justo, y no a lo violento; que nos mande la razón, no el albedrío; [. . .] que seamos cuidado de los príncipes, no mercancía; y en las repúblicas compañeros, y no esclavos; miembros, y no trastos; cuerpos, y no sombra" (Quevedo, *La Hora* 358). But the letrado's recommendations are quickly shown to be impracticable: they are drowned out by the shouts of the multitude, characterized as "trastos" and "sombra," rather than as "miembros" and "cuerpos."

Insofar as the cadaveral condition of all human activity makes the resurrection of the social body impossible, a key function of allegory is lost. Again I turn to Benjamin, this time, his early work on the Trauerspiel, for, through it, we can further comprehend the sense in which Quevedo's condemnation of language ultimately compromises the task of the allegorist. The allegorist described by Benjamin is, like Quevedo, deeply aware of the sense in which the historical process occludes or contaminates the Original Word. But this consciousness makes him capable of stripping away the temporal residue of contingent secondary signification and unveiling primordial meaning: "Origin is still the goal, but not as a fixed image of the past that must be recaptured in toto, but rather as the fulfillment of a potentiality that lies dormant in origin, the attainment of which simultaneously represents a quantum leap beyond the original point of departure. According to this conception, human activity can play a role in the realization of this goal, but since the realms of history and salvation are *antitheses,* human action can never have a *direct* effect in bringing it about" (Wolin 39). Equipped with an understanding of the paradoxical nature of knowledge, the allegorist is capable of overcoming the antithesis between the sacred and the profane. The prominence of corpses in the Trauerspiel recalls the removal from an eternal realm, but, at the same time, Benjamin endows these very corpses with transcendental significance (*The Origin* 217). As Richard Wolin explains,

> for the stylized dramas of the baroque, nature is no longer symbolically represented by serene Olympian deities, but allegorically by a "death's head." [. . .] The meanings of allegorical images are by no means self-evident, for according to the historico-philosophical dynamic of the allegorical world view, *all* meaning has ceased to be self-evident. In this chaotic cosmos of desultory, miscellaneous fragments, the allegorist alone is sovereign. He is responsible for bestowing meaning in an inverted world in which any "person, any object, any relationship can mean absolutely anything else." [. . .] Although the profane world is totally devalued [. . .] insofar as it is in turn read as an allegorical cryptogram of redeemed life, its status is simultaneously elevated. (67–68)

No such elevation is ciphered in *La Hora de todos*. Rather, the allegorist settles for reminding the audience that history mimics the uncontrolled mutability of the Circe-like coin and the arbitrary multiplication of the letter, thereby eluding all stabilizing translation. By engaging in so extreme a reading of changing material reality as an irrevocable decay of communication, Quevedo chooses cultural demise over cultural reinvention. Although such a stance is pitted against the dynamic fusion of cultural sphere, subject, and state formation, which would come to constitute modern aesthetic sensibility (Spadaccini and Talens), *La Hora de todos* is itself a quintessentially modern work. Its profoundly troubled view of the relationship between art and society anticipated a level of conflictedness that would someday come to dominate art, as it imagined its own ending centuries later in an industrialized era.

EPILOGUE

IN A WELL-KNOWN ESSAY, Borges grapples with the question of why Quevedo is omitted from the census of "nombres universales" (*Otras inquisiciones* 59). The essay is often cited by *quevedistas,* especially its last sentence, which provides a remarkably rhetorical solution to the quandary of Quevedo's limited fame: "Quevedo es menos un hombre que una dilatada y compleja literatura" (Borges, *Otras inquisiciones* 70). Other celebrated writers survive, Borges explains, because they have coined a lasting symbol that succeeds in captivating future generations: Homer's Priam humbled before Achilles, Dante's concentric circles of Hell, Cervantes's dialogue between don Quijote and Sancho, Kafka's nightmarish labyrinths. By contrast, Borges finds the symbol that sums up Quevedo—that of consummate stylist—to have far less appeal. Insufficient to ensure his standing as a true classic writer, Quevedo's avid cultivation of the Spanish language in all of its registers, high and low, can only secure him a place in the memory of other literati.

That Quevedo's signal trait is his passionate engagement with language is beyond dispute. But, as we think through the link implied by Borges between the rhetorical nature of Quevedo's authorial enterprise and its lack of universal stature, we must not lose sight of the particular and historically identifiable definition of universality operative in Borges's assessment. The real problem at issue is that the concepts of author and work present in Quevedo's writing clash with the definitions to which Borges's notion of universality is harnessed.

In admitting figures like Dante and Cervantes into the universal pantheon and excluding Quevedo from it, Borges is adhering to twentieth-century analytic parameters that see the meaning of literature as created through the interpretive license of individual readers. The related conceptions of author and work, which themselves must be understood as socially and ideologically constructed categories, have a close affinity with the Barthesian and Foucaultian formulations that would become so influential in the 1970s and 1980s (see Premat). "The mark of the writer is reduced to nothing more than the singularity of his absence," Michel Foucault would say (102–3), converging in many respects with Roland Barthes's pronouncements about the "death of the author" (49). Reacting against the nineteenth-century habit of tethering textual analysis to authorial biography, Borges, like these thinkers, sees himself as freeing literature from constraining determinism. If he integrates Dante and Cervantes without reservation to the world canon, it is because their authorial personae somehow conform to the fictions of authorship judged instrumental to the productive exercise of interpretive subjectivity. Essential to the interpretive autonomy of the reader, these fictions conjure up an idea of unified authorship that makes it possible to avoid the paralyzing prospect of an arbitrary profusion of meanings, as Foucault would say. The fertility of their imaginary worlds is tied to their yielding an iconic synthesis, an impression of wholeness. Divergently, Borges portrays Quevedo's corpus as being without unity, an agglomeration of circumstantial rhetorical poses. Hence Quevedo's authorial persona is not quite reconcilable with reading understood as a seamless and intimate interaction with an infinite imagined universe.

As I have shown, a connecting thread in Quevedo's prose corpus is its focus on communication. That is what sets his works apart from Borges's other classics. Writing in an era that lays intellectual and cultural foundations crucial to the emergence of the eighteenth-century "detached" subject (e.g., humanism, picaresque narrative, spiritual confession, courtly discretion, political pragmatism, the scientific revolution, disciplinary divisions, print culture), Quevedo holds on to a conception of verbal transmission that is reactionary even for his own time, aspiring as it does for the word to wield a supreme social and political role. Whereas in Borges's silent and anonymous literary universe, the untroubled reader is charged with conferring meaning, in Quevedo's universe, the texts actively seek to overwhelm their audience. In their eucharistic conception of the ideal word, in their contentiousness toward the unfettered expansion of communication beyond the corporeal control of sacralized authority, Quevedo's prose works place inordinate emphasis on the originary act of communication. As vividly demonstrated through the messianic exhibitions of royal might found in *Política de Dios* and through episodes from *Marco Bruto,* such as those depicting Brutus writing in the midst of battle, Mark Antony captivating the crowd, or Cicero defying his assassins, Quevedo is loath to separate the act of reception from the sensorial influence of live transmission. The meaning of words is, by his standards, entirely harnessed to their imagined existence as performed utterances. The pronounced kinship between the conceptions of text advanced in Quevedo's writings and the synesthetic experience summoned in the oratorical, pictorial, and ceremonial practices of Tridentine Church and state bespeaks a deliberate stance against the explosion of print culture. As *La Hora de todos* makes clear, far from allowing for the possibility of interpretive density to be gained from a growing public sphere, Quevedo lambastes the nascent versions of the autonomous modern subject.

It is not that Quevedo is "less a man" than a "complex literature." Rather, it is that the complexity of his conflicted identification with the republic of letters registers itself in his writings. Though he was, in many senses, a quintessential man of letters, a creature of print culture—what more proof than his famous poem beginning "Retirado en la paz de estos desiertos, con pocos, / pero doctos libros juntos"? (*Antología* 99)—he tenaciously resisted Spain's emergence as "racionalmente moderna, precapitalista y escritófila" (Bouza, *Del escribano* 24). Fully aware that the ongoing changes in literary production and transmission were unstoppable, he continued to defend body-centered models of eloquence in the strongest of terms. Hence his prose can be said to sit somewhat uncomfortably in the world of silent reading.

But today, given the increased attention paid to the relationship between literary texts and other cultural mediums, Quevedo's fusion of writing and performance, though certainly remarkable in degree, should no longer pose an analytic dilemma. Far from a peripheral or dated preoccupation, his concern with the effects of historical change on how writing as both material and conceptual activity is imagined signifies an engagement with the question of what authorship and readership mean, a question that continues to be of central pertinence to the twenty-first century.

NOTES

INTRODUCTION

1. An indispensable reference on contextualizing Quevedo's political program is Lía Schwartz Lerner and Antonio Carreira's anthology *Quevedo a nueva luz*.

2. "It is true that, so long as I merely considered the customs of other men, I found hardly anything there about which to be confident, and that I noticed there was about as much diversity as I had previously found among the opinions of philosophers. Thus, the greatest profit I derived from this was that, on seeing many things that, although they seem to us very extravagant and ridiculous, do not cease to be commonly accepted and approved among other great peoples, I learned not to believe anything too firmly of which I had been persuaded only by example and custom" (Descartes 6).

3. Spelling and punctuation in the quotations from early modern sources have not been modernized throughout: I have respected the variations present in the specific editions cited.

CHAPTER 1

1. For an earlier version of the argument made in this chapter and in chapter 2, see my article "All the Court's a Stage." I am grateful to the *Journal of Spanish Cultural Studies* (http://www.informaworld.com) for granting me permission to reproduce some of its content here.

2. With respect to the French ancien régime, which is comparable to the Spanish antiguo régimen as concerns the powers of the sovereign's word and presence, see Apostolidès on how the state machine encroaches on the king's authority (*Le roi-machine* 131). For treatment of this subject within the Spanish context, see González Enciso.

3. On the dates of the manuscripts and first editions of parts I and II, consult James Crosby's introduction to *Política de Dios* (14).

4. Although Philip IV (r. 1621–40) would, like his predecessor, turn out to be a weak monarch, with Olivares tending to monopolize important decision making, it is crucial to bear in mind the significant differences between the political programs of the two regimes (Stradling 59–60), especially given that part I of Quevedo's treatise reflects the aspirations of the new regime. Furthermore, at this time, the failings of Olivares's statesmanship had not yet made themselves felt.

5. For solid commentary and identification of the innumerable biblical citations contained in *Política de Dios,* consult Crosby's indispensable notes to his edition of the work (463–512). As is evident there and in the excerpts from Matthew cited below, Quevedo took considerable liberties with his biblical quotations. Although the Latin quotations and his own Spanish translations can be identified with the authorized Sistine and Clementine Vulgate Bibles published in Rome in the 1590s, because Quevedo's wording is not always faithful to the original, which edition or editions he used cannot be determined for certain.

6. Berger distinguishes "between two hypothetical orders of communication and semiosis—one centered on speaker and hearer, the other on reader and writer. In the first, all messages—nonverbal as well as verbal—are transmitted through the channel of the body and its extensions, while in the second, all messages are abstracted from the body and reconstructed in graphic media so they can pass through written channels" (147).

7. Given the general dearth of more recent studies on Spanish mirrors of princes, María Angeles Galino Carrillo's overview of the genre continues to be a relevant, though limited, reference. For more current and thorough treatments of the genre, in the European context, see Bireley and Meyer, although neither work focuses on questions of political communication. For a solid historical analysis of early modern Spanish kingship, see also Feros, *Kingship*.

8. "There is some danger of our being more impressed by the workings of a propaganda machine than were those at whom it was directed, simply because of the quantity of evidence left behind for later generations" (Elliott, "The Court" 163).

9. "Another example of the Christianization of the classical past is the retelling of the *Argonautica* narrative in terms of a Biblical story of rebirth. Through that form of syncretistic Christian thought which sought to amalgamate the sacred and profane, the ram's celestial reappearance that heralded the returning Golden Age was identified with Christ's restoration of the state of innocence that existed in Eden before the Fall. What is more, the beginning and the end of Christian time are accorded in this sign. Announced in the heavens since the creation, Aries marks the seasonal moment of Incarnation. Each year at Eastertide, Aries returns to announce its Eucharistic message and to reiterate Saint John's apocalyptic promise. Thus, in Christian thought, the whole cycle of Redemption—the beginning of Christ's life on earth and the sign of his sacrifice and return—cohere in this cosmic icon" (Tanner 149).

10. On the pragmatic bent of the Spanish anti-Machiavellians, see Bireley 239. Although it claims to break with the legacy of the Florentine thinker, anti-Machiavellian thought is equally concerned with the efficacious projection of authority.

11. The English-language biblical quotations in this and chapter 2 are taken from *The New Oxford Annotated Bible* (1994).

12. Quevedo's disparaging reference to the pen is charged with meaning in the context of the Habsburg state apparatus, which was so reliant on the written word for its day-to-day operations, an issue I shall return to in chapter 4.

13. Although this quotation is actually in part II of *Política de Dios*, I include it here because it amply describes the work as a whole.

CHAPTER 2

1. On the differences between the political agendas of the two parts of *Política de Dios*, see Edwards.

2. On Caravaggio's rendering of physical violence, see Bal 30–32.

3. Quevedo emphatically adds, "Quien os dixere, que vos no podeis hacer estos Milagros, dar vista, y pies, y vida, y salud, y resurreccion, y libertad de oppression de malos espiritus, esse os quiere ciego, y tullido, y muerto, y enfermo, y posseido de su mal espiritu" (*Política* 165).

CHAPTER 3

1. For an initial approach to the argument made in this chapter, see my article "On Rulership and Conspiracy in Quevedo's *Marco Bruto*." I thank *Confluencia* for granting me permission to reproduce part of its content here.

2. On *Marco Bruto*'s political pragmatism, see Peraita, "From Plutarch's Glossator," and Blanco 529. The treatise's rhetorical import has not received sustained attention beyond Krabbenhoft's study, which productively situates it within curial rhetorical and social conventions but does not attend to the sense in which *Marco Bruto* questions these conventions.

3. "Ramist rhetoric belongs to a critical period in the history of these Western *artes sermonicales,* and suggests interrelationships between developments in these arts and the development of letterpress printing, the perfecting of the textbook, the burgeoning of a potentially infinite number of 'courses' or 'subjects' in the curriculum, and finally the emergence of modern science itself" (Ong, *Ramus* 288).

4. On Quevedo's political career, see Elliott, "Quevedo."

5. On the thematic unity of *Marco Bruto,* see Martinengo.

6. On Quevedo's 1629 letter as a means of political alliance building, see Elías Rivers's introduction to "Dedicatoria."

CHAPTER 4

1. For an initial version of the argument made in this chapter, see my article "The Demise of Eloquence and the Cult of Spectacle in Quevedo's *La Hora de todos.*" I thank the *Bulletin of Hispanic Studies* for granting me permission to reproduce some of its content here.

2. On the dates of the manuscripts and first editions of *La Hora de todos,* consult Bourg, Dupont, and Geneste 122–32.

3. Although situated in Denmark, the vignette on the arbitristas in *La Hora* ch 18 can be understood as a commentary on Spanish society, given the iconic status of the arbitrista in Spain.

4. For a revisionist view on the assumed gap between literacy rates in Spain and northern Europe, see Nolle.

WORKS CITED

Agamben, Giorgio. *Homo Sacer: Sovereign Power and Bare Life*. Stanford: Stanford University Press, 1998.
———. *The Man Without Content*. Stanford: Stanford University Press, 1999.
———. *The Open: Man and Animal*. Stanford: Stanford University Press, 2004.
Álamos de Barrientos, Baltasar. *Aforismos al Tácito español*. 1614. Madrid: Centro de Estudios Constitucionales, 1987.
———. *Discurso político al rey Felipe III al comienzo de su reinado*. 1598. Barcelona: Anthropos, 1990.
Apostolidès, Jean-Marie. *Le prince sacrifié: Théâtre et politique au temps de Louis XIV.* Paris: Editions de Minuit, 1985.
———. *Le roi-machine: Spectacle et politique au temps de Louis XIV.* Paris: Éditions Minuit, 1981.
Aristotle. *On Rhetoric: A Theory of Civic Discourse*. Trans. George A. Kennedy. New York: Oxford University Press, 1991.
Athanasius the Great. *The Life of St. Anthony the Great*. Willits, Calif.: Orthodox, 1994.
Augustine of Hippo. *On Christian Teaching*. Trans. and ed. R. P. H. Green. Oxford: Oxford University Press, 1997.
———. *Confessions*. Trans. and ed. H. Chadwick. Oxford: Oxford University Press, 1991.
———. *The First Catechetical Instruction*. Trans. Joseph P. Christopher. Westminster, Md.: Newman, 1946.
Ávila, Juan de. *Por qué quema el fuego: Lecciones de un maestro de la vida espiritual*. 1595. Madrid: Ediciones Paulinas, 1991.
Bal, Mieke. *Quoting Caravaggio: Contemporary Art, Preposterous History*. Chicago: Chicago University Press, 1999.
Barthes, Roland. *The Rustle of Language*. Trans. Richard Howard. Berkeley and Los Angeles: University of California Press, 1989.
Beaudrillard, Jean. *Simulacra and Simulation*. Trans. Sheila Faria Glaser. Ann Arbor: University of Michigan Press, 1994.
Benjamin, Walter. *The Origin of German Tragic Drama*. Trans. John Osborne. Norfolk: Lowe and Brydone, 1977.
———. "The Work of Art in the Age of Mechanical Reproduction." *Illuminations*. Trans. Harry Zohn. Ed. Hannah Arendt. New York: Harcourt Brace Jovanovich, 1968. 217–51.
Berger, Harry. "Bodies and Texts." *Representations* 17 (1987): 145–64.

Bernat Vistarini, Antonio, John T. Cull, and Edward J. Vodoklys, eds. *Enciclopedia de emblemas españoles ilustrados*. Madrid: Akal, 1999.
Bertelli, Sergio. *The King's Body: Sacred Rituals of Power in Medieval and Early Modern Europe*. University Park: Pennsylvania State University Press, 2001.
Bireley, Robert. *The Counter-Reformation Prince: Anti-Machiavellianism or Catholic Statecraft in Early Modern Europe*. Chapel Hill: University of North Carolina Press, 1990.
Blanco, Mercedes. *Les rhétoriques de la pointe: Baltasar Gracián et le conceptisme en Europe*. Genève: Slatkine, 1992.
Bloch, Marc. *Les rois thaumaturges: Étude sur le caractère surnaturel attribué à la puissance royale particulièrement en France et en Angleterre*. Paris: Gallimard, 1983.
Borges, Jorge Luis. *Inquisiciones*. Buenos Aires: Seix Barral, 1993.
———. *Otras inquisiciones*. Buenos Aires: Emecé, 1996.
Borja, Juan de. *Empresas morales*. 1581. Madrid: Fundación Universitaria Española, 1981.
Borromeo, Carlo. *Instructiones praedicationis verbi Dei, et confessariorom*. Brescia: Joannes Baptista Grumus, 1676.
Bourdieu, Pierre. "From the King's House to the Reason of State: A Model of the Genesis of the Bureaucratic Field." *Pierre Bourdieu and Democratic Politics: The Mystery of Ministry*. Ed. Loïc Wacquant. Cambridge: Polity Press, 2005. 28–54.
———. *Language and Symbolic Power*. Trans. Gino Raymond and Matthew Adamson. Ed. John B. Thompson. Cambridge, Mass.: Harvard University Press, 1991.
Bourg, Jean, Pierre Dupont, and Pierre Geneste. "Introducción." *La Hora de todos y la Fortuna con seso*. Francisco de Quevedo y Villegas. Ed. Jean Bourg, Pierre Dupont, and Pierre Geneste. Madrid: Cátedra, 1987. 13–143.
Bouza, Fernando. *Communication, Knowledge, and Memory*. Trans. Sonia López and Michael Agnew. Philadelphia: University of Pennsylvania Press, 2004.
———. *Corre manuscrito: Una historia cultural del Siglo de Oro*. Madrid: Marcial Pons, 2001.
———. *Del escribano a la biblioteca: La civilización escrita europea en la alta edad moderna (siglos XV–XVII)*. Madrid: Síntesis, 1997.
———. *Imagen y propaganda: Capítulos de historia cultural del reinado de Felipe II*. Madrid: Akal, 1998.
Brown, Jonathan. *Velázquez: Painter and Courtier*. New Haven: Yale University Press, 1986.
Brown, Jonathan, and John H. Elliott. *A Palace for a King: The Buen Retiro and the Court of Philip IV*. New Haven: Yale University Press, 1980.
Brown, Peter. *The Cult of the Saints: Its Rise and Function in Latin Christianity*. Chicago: University of Chicago Press, 1981.
Burke, Peter. *The Fabrication of Louis XIV*. New Haven: Yale University Press, 1992.
———. *A Social History of Knowledge*. Cambridge: Polity, 2000.
Calderón de la Barca, Pedro. *El médico de su honra*. Ed. D. W. Cruickshank. Madrid: Castalia, 1989.
———. *El nuevo palacio del Retiro*. Ed. Alan K. G. Paterson. Pamplona: Universidad de Navarra, 1998.
———. *La vida es sueño*. Ed. Domingo Ynduráin. Madrid: Biblioteca Nueva, 2004.
Calinescu, Matei. *Five Faces of Modernity: Modernism, Avant-Garde, Decadence, Kitsch, Postmodernism*. Durham: Duke University Press, 1987.

Campanella, Tommaso. *Monarchie d'Espagne et monarchie de France*. Paris: Presses Universitaires de France, 1997.
Cascardi, Anthony. *The Subject of Modernity*. Cambridge: Cambridge University Press, 1992.
Castiglione, Baldesar. *The Book of the Courtier*. Trans. Charles S. Singleton. New York: Doubleday, 1959.
Caussin, Nicolas. *La Cour sainte*. Paris: Sebastien Chappelet, 1625.
Chartier, Roger. *Entre poder y placer: Cultura escrita y literatura en la edad moderna*. Trans. Maribel García Sánchez. Madrid: Catedra, 2000.
———. *On the Edge of the Cliff*. Trans. Lydia G. Cochrane. Baltimore: Johns Hopkins University Press, 1997.
Cicero, Marcus Tullius. *Orator*. Ed. P. Reis. Stuttgart: Teubner, 1963.
Clamurro, William. "Empire and Marginality in *La Hora de todos*." *Studies in Honor of James O. Crosby*. Ed. Lía Schwartz Lerner. Newark: Juan de la Cuesta, 2004. 91–108.
———. *Language and Ideology in the Prose of Quevedo*. Newark: Juan de la Cuesta, 1991.
Coleridge, Samuel Taylor. *The Statesman's Manual: Lay Sermons*. London: Routledge, 1972.
de Armas, Frederick A. *Cervantes, Raphael, and the Classics*. Cambridge: Cambridge University Press, 1998.
———. *Quixotic Frescoes: Cervantes and Italian Renaissance Art*. Toronto: University of Toronto Press, 2006.
———, ed. *Writing for the Eyes in the Spanish Golden Age*. Lewisburg: Bucknell University Press, 2004.
de Man, Paul. "The Rhetoric of Temporality." *Blindness and Insight: Essays in the Rhetoric of Contemporary Criticism*. Paul de Man. Minneapolis: University of Minnesota Press, 1983. 187–228.
Derrida, Jacques. *De la Grammatologie*. Paris: Minuit, 1967.
Descartes, René. *Discourse on Method*. 1637. Trans. and ed. Donald A. Cress. Indianapolis: Hackett, 1998.
Durán, Manuel. *Francisco de Quevedo*. Madrid: EDAF, 1978.
Edwards, Richard. "*Govierno de Christo* and *Tyrania de Satanas*: The Differences Between Parts I and II of Francisco de Quevedo's *Política de Dios*." *Bulletin of Hispanic Studies* 76 (1999): 605–26.
Elias, Norbert. *The Civilizing Process: Sociogenetic and Psychogenetic Investigations*. Trans. Edmund Jephcott. London: Blackwell, 2004.
———. *The Court Society*. Trans. Edmund Jephcott. New York: Pantheon, 1983.
Elliott, John H. *The Count-Duke of Olivares: The Statesman in an Age of Decline*. New Haven: Yale University Press, 1986.
———. "The Court of the Spanish Habsburgs: A Peculiar Institution?" *Spain and Its World, 1500–1700*. Ed. John H. Elliott. New Haven: Yale University Press, 1989. 142–61.
———. *Imperial Spain, 1469–1716*. London: Penguin, 1963.
———. "Quevedo and the Count-Duke of Olivares." *Quevedo in Perspective*. Ed. James Iffland. Newark: Juan de La Cuesta, 1980. 227–50.
Erasmus, Desiderius. *The Education of a Christian Prince*. Trans. Neil M. Cheshire and Michael J. Heath. Cambridge: Cambridge University Press, 1997.
———. *The Praise of Folly*. Trans. Clarence H. Miller. New Haven: Yale University Press, 1979.

Ettinghausen, Henry. "Politics and the Press in Spain." *The Politics of Information in Early Modern Europe*. Ed. Brendan Dooley and Sabrina Baron. London: Routledge, 2001. 119–50.
Fayard, Janine. *Les membres du conseil de Castille à l'époque moderne (1621–1746)*. Geneva: Droz, 1979.
Fernández, Luis Gil. *Panorama social del humanismo español (1500–1800)*. Madrid: Tecnos, 1997.
Fernández López, Jorge. "Rhetorical Theory in Sixteenth-Century Spain: A Critical Survey." *Rhetorica* 20.2 (2002): 133–48.
Fernández Santamaría, José. *Razón de estado y política en el pensamiento español del barroco (1595–1640)*. Madrid: Centro de Estudios Constitucionales, 1986.
Feros, Antonio. *Kingship and Favoritism in the Spain of Philip III, 1598–1621*. Cambridge: Cambridge University Press, 2000.
———. "'Sacred and Terrifying Gazes': Languages and Images of Power in Early Modern Spain." *The Cambridge Companion to Velázquez*. Ed. Suzanne Stratton-Pruitt. Cambridge: Cambridge University Press, 2002. 68–86.
Forcione, Alban K. "At the Threshold of Modernity: Gracián's *El criticón*." *Rhetoric and Politics: Baltasar Gracián and the New World Order*. Ed. Nicholas Spadaccini and Jenaro Talens. Minneapolis: University of Minnesota Press, 1997. 3–70.
———. *Majesty and Humanity: Kings and Their Doubles in the Political Drama of the Spanish Golden Age*. New Haven: Yale University Press, 2009.
Foucault, Michel. "What Is an Author?" *The Foucault Reader*. Ed. Paul Rabinow. New York: Pantheon, 1984. 101–13.
Freedberg, David. *The Power of Images: Studies in the History and Theory of Response*. Chicago: University of Chicago Press, 1989.
Fumaroli, Marc. *L'age de l'éloquence: Rhétorique et 'res literaria' de la Renaissance au seuil de l'époque classique*. Geneva: Droz, 1980.
Gadamer, Hans Georg. *Truth and Method*. Trans. W. Glen-Doepel; rev. Joel Weinsheimer and Donald G. Marshall. Ed. Garrett Barden and John Cumming. New York: Crossroad, 1988.
Galino Carrillo, María Angeles. *Los tratados sobre educación de príncipes, siglos XVI y XVII*. Madrid: Consejo Superior de Investigaciones Científicas, 1948.
Gallego, Julián. *Visión y símbolos en la pintura española del siglo de oro*. Madrid: Cátedra, 1987.
García-Bryce, Ariadna. "All the Court's a Stage: Performing Piety in Quevedo's *Política de Dios*." *Journal of Spanish Cultural Studies* 6.3 (2005): 271–85.
———. "The Demise of Eloquence and the Cult of Spectacle in Quevedo's *La Hora de todos*." *Bulletin of Hispanic Studies* 82 (2005): 313–25.
———. "Envisioning the Body Politic: Iconographies of Christian Rulership." *Imagery, Spirituality and Ideology in Baroque Spain and Latin America*. Ed. Jeremy Roe and Marta Bustillo. Newcastle upon Tyne: Cambridge Scholars, 2010. 15–28.
———. "On Rulership and Conspiracy in Quevedo's *Marco Bruto*." *Confluencia* 18.2 (2003): 182–95.
García Santo-Tomás, Enrique. *Espacio urbano y creación literaria en el Madrid de Felipe IV*. Madrid: Universidad de Navarra, 2004.
Gauger, Hans-Martin. "La conciencia lingüística del Siglo de Oro." *Actas del IX Congreso de la Asociación Internacional de Hispanistas*. Ed. Sebastián Neumeister. Frankfurt am Main: Vervuert, 1989. 45–63.

Geertz, Clifford. "Religion as a Cultural System." *Reader in Comparative Religion*. Ed. William A. Lessa and Evon Z. Vogt. New York: Harper and Row, 1965. 204–16.
Goffman, Erving. *The Presentation of Self in Everyday Life*. Garden City: Doubleday, 1959.
Gómez de la Reguera, Francisco. *Empresas de los reyes de Castilla y de León*. 1632. Valladolid: Universidad de Valladolid, 1990.
González Dávila, Gil. *Teatro eclesiástico de la primitiva iglesia de la Nueva España en las Indias Occidentales*. Madrid: J. Porrúa Turanzas, 1959.
González de Cellorigo, Martín. *Memorial de la política necessaria, y útil restauración a la República de España, y estados de ella, y del desempeño universal de estos reynos*. Madrid: Instituto de Cooperación Iberoamericana, 1991.
González Enciso, Agustín. "Del rey ausente al rey distante." *Imagen del rey, imagen de los reinos: Las ceremonias públicas en la España Moderna (1500–1814)*. Ed. Agustín González Enciso and Jesús María Usunáriz Garayoa. Pamplona: Universidad de Navarra, 1999. 1–18.
Gracián, Baltasar. *Agudeza y arte de ingenio*. 1648. Ed. Evaristo Correa Calderón. 2 vols. Madrid: Castalia, 1987.
———. *El héroe* (1637); *El discreto* (1646); *Oráculo manual y arte de prudencia* (1647). Ed. Luys Santa Marina. Barcelona: Planeta, 1996.
Granada, Luis de. *De la retórica eclesiástica*. 1576. *Obras de Fray Luis de Granada*. Madrid: Atlas, 1945. 488–642.
Greer, Margaret Rich. "Constituting Community: A New Historical Perspective on the Autos of Calderón." *New Historicism and the Comedia: Poetics, Politics, and Praxis*. Ed. José Madrigal. Boulder: Society of Spanish and Spanish American Studies, 1997. 41–67.
———. *The Play of Power: Mythological Court Dramas of Calderón de la Barca*. Princeton: Princeton University Press, 1991.
Guevara, Antonio de. *Menosprecio de corte y alabanza de aldea*. 1539. Madrid: Cátedra, 1987.
———. *Relox de príncipes*. 1529. *Obras completas de Fray Antonio de Guevara*. Vol. 2. Madrid: Fundación José Antonio de Castro, 1994.
Gutiérrez, Carlos. *La espada, el rayo, y la pluma: Quevedo y los campos literario y de poder*. West Lafayette: Purdue University Press, 2005.
Hampton, Timothy. "Difficult Engagements: Private Passion and Public Service in Montaigne's *Essais*." *Politics and the Passions, 1500–1850*. Ed. Victoria Kahn, Neil Saccamano, and Daniela Coli. Princeton: Princeton University Press, 2006. 30–48.
Harvey, Elizabeth D., ed. *Sensible Flesh: On Touch in Early Modern Culture*. Philadelphia: University of Pennsylvania Press, 2003.
Heiple, Daniel. *Mechanical Imagery in Spanish Golden Age Poetry*. Potomac: Studia Humanitatis, 1983.
Herrera, Fernando de. "Poética." 1580. *Poesía y poética de Fernando de Herrera*. Ed. Manuel Ángel Vásquez. Madrid: Narcea, 1983. 136–91.
Hillman, David, and Carla Mazzio, eds. *The Body in Parts: Fantasies of Corporeality in Early Modern Europe*. New York: Routledge, 1997.
Hobbes, Thomas. *Leviathan*. 1651. Ed. Richard Tuck. Cambridge: Cambridge University Press, 1991.
Huarte de San Juan, Juan. *Examen de ingenios*. 1575. Madrid: Cátedra, 1989.

Hutson, Lorna. "Not the King's Two Bodies: Reading the 'Body Politic' in Shakespeare's *Henry IV*, Parts I and 2." *Rhetoric and Law in Early Modern Europe*. New Haven: Yale University Press, 2001. 166–98.
Iffland, James. "Apocalypse Later: Ideology and Quevedo's *La Hora de todos*." *Revista de Estudios Hispanicos* 7 (1980): 87–132.
———. *Quevedo and the Grostesque*. London: Tamesis, 1978.
Ignatius of Loyola. *The Spiritual Exercises of St. Ignatius*. Trans. Anthony Mottola. Garden City, N.Y.: Image Books, 1964.
Jáuregui y Aguilar, Juan de. *Discurso poético*. 1624. Madrid: Editora Nacional, 1978.
Juan de la Cruz. *Poesía*. 1618. Ed. Domingo Ynduráin. Madrid: Catédra, 2002.
Kagan, Richard. *Lawsuits and Litigants in Castile, 1500–1700*. Chapel Hill: University of North Carolina Press, 1981.
Kahn, Victoria. "The Passions and the Interests in Early Modern Europe: The Case of Guarini's *Il Pastor fido*." *Reading the Early Modern Passions: Essays in the Cultural History of Emotion*. Ed. Gail Kern Paster, Katherine Rowe, and Mary Floyd-Wilson. Philadelphia: University of Pennsylvania Press, 2004. 217–39.
Kahn, Victoria, and Neil Saccamano. "Introduction." *Politics and the Passions, 1500–1850*. Ed. Victoria Kahn, Neil Saccamano, and Daniela Coli. Princeton: Princeton University Press, 2006. 1–6.
Kamen, Henry. *Golden Age Spain*. Hampshire: Palgrave Macmillan, 2005.
———. *Spain in the Later Seventeenth Century, 1665–1700*. London: Longman, 1980.
Kantorowicz, Ernst. *The King's Two Bodies: A Study in Medieval Political Theology*. Princeton: Princeton University Press, 1957.
Kern Paster, Gail, Katherine Rowe, and Mary Floyd-Wilson, eds. *Reading the Early Modern Passions: Essays in the Cultural History of Emotion*. Philadelphia: University of Pennsylvania Press, 2004.
Kertzer, David. *Ritual, Politics, and Power*. New Haven: Yale University Press, 1988.
King, Nathalia. "The Mind's Eye and the Forms of Thought: Classical Rhetoric and the Composition of Augustine's Confessions." Ph.D. diss., New York University, 1991.
Kléber Monod, Paul. *The Power of Kings: Monarchy and Religion in Europe, 1589–1715*. New Haven: Yale University Press, 1999.
Krabbenhoft, Kenneth. *El precio de la cortesía: Retórica e innovación en Quevedo y Gracián: Un estudio de la "Vida de Marco Bruto" y del "Oráculo manual y arte de prudencia."* Salamanca: Universidad de Salamanca, 1994.
La Flor, Fernando. *Barroco: Representación e ideología en el mundo hispánico, 1580–1680*. Fernando R. de la Flor. Madrid: Cátedra, 2002.
Láinez, José. *El privado christiano: Deducido de las Vidas de Ioseph y Daniel, que fueron Valanzas de los validos*. Madrid: Imprenta del Reyno, 1641.
Lascombes, André. "Image et culture commune à la Renaissance: De quelques exemples anglais et français." *Spectacle and Image in Renaissance Europe*. Leiden: Brill, 1993. 9–31.
Ledda, Giuseppina. *La parola e l'immagine: Strategie della persuasione religiosa nella Spagna secentesca*. Pisa: ETS, 2003.
Lequile, A. F. Diego da. *Colossvs Angelicvs, Avstriacvs, sive Avstriae Sobolis admiranda moles Apocalypsea, Religione constans*. Oeniponti [Innsbruck]: Hieronymus Agricola, 1655.
Lewis, Tom, and Francisco J. Sánchez, eds. *Culture and the State in Spain*. New York: Garland, 1999.

Lezra, Jacques. *Unspeakable Subjects: The Genealogy of the Event in Early Modern Europe*. Stanford: Stanford University Press, 1997.
Lida, Raimundo. *Prosas de Quevedo*. Barcelona: Editorial Crítica, 1980.
Lipsius, Justus. *Principles of Letter-Writing*. 1591. Trans. R. V. Young and M. Thomas Hester. Carbondale: Southern Illinois University Press, 1996.
Lisón Tolosana, Carmelo. *La imagen del rey: Monarquía, realeza y poder ritual en la Casa de los Austrias*. Madrid: Espasa Calpe, 1991.
Longinus. *On the Sublime*. Trans. James A. Arieti and John. M. Crosset. New York: Mellen, 1985.
López, Roberto J. "Ceremonia y poder en el Antiguo Régimen. Algunas reflexiones sobre fuentes y perspectivas de análisis." *Imagen del rey, imagen de los reinos: Las ceremonias públicas en la España Moderna (1500–1814)*. Ed. Agustín González Enciso and Jesús María Usunáriz Garayoa. Pamplona: Universidad de Navarra, 1999. 19–61.
López Grigera, Luisa. *La retórica en la España del siglo de oro: Teoría y práctica*. Salamanca: Universidad de Salamanca, 1994.
Malvezzi, Virgilio. *Il ritratti del privato politico cristiano*. Palermo: Sellerio, 1993.
Maravall, Antonio. *La cultura del barroco*. Barcelona: Ariel, 1983.
Mariana, Juan de. *La dignidad real y la educación del rey (De rege et regis institutione)*. 1598. Madrid: Centro de Estudios Constitucionales, 1981.
Marin, Louis. *Portrait of the King*. Trans. Martha M. Houle. Minneapolis: University of Minnesota Press, 1988.
Mariscal, George. *Contradictory Subjects: Quevedo, Cervantes, and Seventeenth-Century Spanish Culture*. Ithaca: Cornell University Press, 1991.
Márquez, Juan. *El governador christiano dedvcido de las vidas de Moysen, y Iosve, principes del pveblo de Dios*. Salamanca: Francisco de Cea Tesa, 1612.
Martinengo, Alessandro. *El "Marco Bruto" de Quevedo: Una unidad en dinámica transformación*. Bern: Peter Lang, 1998.
Mártir Rizo, Juan Pablo. *Norte de príncipes*. Madrid: Centro de Estudios Constitucionales, 1988.
McLuhan, Marshall. *The Gutenberg Galaxy: The Making of Typographic Man*. Toronto: University of Toronto Press, 1962.
Meyer, Jean. *L'éducation des princes du XVe au XIXe siècle*. Paris: Perrin, 2004.
Moncada, Sancho de. *Restauración política de España*. 1619. Madrid: Instituto de Estudios Fiscales, 1974.
Most, Glenn. *Doubting Thomas*. Cambridge, Mass.: Harvard University Press, 2005.
Mouchel, Christian. "Les rhétoriques post-tridentines (1570–1600): La fabrique d'une société chrétienne." *Histoire de la rhétorique dans l'Europe moderne (1450–1950)*. Ed. Marc Fumaroli. Paris: Presses Universitaires de France, 1999. 431–97.
Mujica Pinilla, Ramón. "El arte y los sermones." *El barroco peruano*. Ed. Pierre Duviols et al. Lima: Banco de Crédito, 2002. 219–306.
Mulryne, J. R., and Elizabeth Goldring, eds. *Court Festivals of the European Renaissance: Art, Politics, and Performance*. Aldershot: Ashgate, 2002.
Mulryne, J. R., Helen Watanabe-O'Kelly, and Margaret Shewring, eds. *Europa Triumphans: Court and Civic Festivals in Early Modern Europe*. Aldershot: Ashgate, 2004.
Nadal, Jerome. *Annotations and Meditations on the Gospels (Adnotationes et meditationes in Evangelio)*. Trans. Frederick J. Homann. Vol. 1. Philadelphia: St. Joseph's Press, 2003.

Navarrete, Ignacio. *Orphans of Petrarch: Poetry and Theory in the Spanish Renaissance*. Berkeley and Los Angeles: University of California Press, 1994.
The New Oxford Annotated Bible. Ed. Bruce M. Metzger and Roland E. Murphy. Oxford: Oxford University Press, 1994.
Nolle, Sarah. "Literacy and Culture in Early Modern Castile." *Past and Present* 125.1 (1989): 65–96.
Núñez de Castro, Alonso. *Libro histórico politico, sólo Madrid es corte, y el cortesano en Madrid*. Madrid: Roque Rico de Miranda, 1675.
Olivares, Gaspar de Guzmán. *Memoriales y cartas del Conde Duque de Olivares*. Ed. J. H. Elliott and José F. de la Peña. Vol. 1. Madrid: Alfaguara, 1978.
Ong, Walter. *Orality and Literacy: The Technologizing of the Word*. London: Routledge, 1982.
———. *Ramus, Method, and the Decay of Dialogue: From the Art of Discourse to the Art of Reason*. Chicago: University of Chicago Press, 2004.
Ortega y Gasset, José. *La rebelión de las masas*. Madrid: Espasa-Calpe, 1964.
Pacheco, Francisco. *El arte de la pintura*. 1649. Madrid: Cátedra, 2001.
———. *Libro de descripción de verdaderos retratos de ilustres y memorables varones*. 1599. Seville: Diputación provincial de Sevilla, 1985.
Pagden, Anthony. *Lords of All the World: Ideologies of Empire in Spain, Britain, and France, c.1500–c.1800*. New Haven: Yale University Press, 1995.
Palafox y Mendoza, Juan de. *Historia real sagrada: Luz de príncipes y súbditos. Obras del ilustrissimo excelentissimo, y venerable siervo de Dios, Don Juan Palafox y Mendoza*. Madrid: Gabriel Ramírez, 1762. 269–664.
Paravicino, Hortensio. *Sermones cortesanos*. Madrid: Castalia, 1994.
Paterson, Alan K. G. "Introducción." *El nuevo palacio del Retiro*. Pedro Calderón de la Barca. Pamplona: Universidad de Navarra, 1998. 11–62.
Peraita, Carmen. "From Plutarch's Glossator to Court Historiographer: Quevedo's Interpretive Strategies in *Vida de Marco Bruto*." *Allegorica* 17 (1996): 73–94.
———. "La oreja, lengua, voz, el grito y las alegorías del acceso al rey: Elocuencia sacra y afectos políticos en *Política de Dios* de Quevedo." *La Perinola* 5 (2001): 185–205.
———. *Quevedo y el joven Felipe IV: El príncipe cristiano y el arte del consejo*. Kassel: Reichenberger, 1997.
Perelman, Chaïm. *Le champ de l'argumentation*. Brussels: Presses Universitaires de Bruxelles, 1970.
Pérez, Joseph. *De l'humanisme aux Lumières: Études sur l'Espagne et l'Amérique*. Madrid: Casa de Velázquez, 2000.
Pérez de Ledesma, Gonzalo. *Censura de la elocuencia*. 1648. Madrid: Crotalón, 1985.
Plato. *Gorgias. The Dialogues of Plato*. Trans. B. Jowett. Vol. 2. London: Oxford University Press, 1953. 501–627.
Pocock, J. G. A. *The Machiavellian Moment: Florentine Political Thought and the Atlantic Republican Tradition*. Princeton: Princeton University Press, 1975.
Poggioli, Renato. *The Theory of the Avant-Garde*. Cambridge, Mass.: Harvard University Press, 1968.
Portocarrero y Guzmán, Pedro. *Teatro monárquico de España*. Madrid: Centro de Estudios Constitucionales, 1998.
Premat, Julio. "Epílogo." *Figuras de Autor: Cahiers de LIRICO* 1 (2006): 311–22.

Pulgar, Hernando del. *Claros varones de Castilla*. 1486. Oxford: Clarendon, 1971.
Pye, Christopher. "The Sovereign, the Theater, and the Kingdome of Darknesse: Hobbes and the Spectacle of Power." *Representations* 8 (1984): 84–106.
Quevedo y Villegas, Francisco de. *Antología poética*. Ed. Pablo Jauraldo Pou. Madrid: Espasa Calpe, 2002.
———. "Carta del Rey don Fernando el Católico al primer virrey de Nápoles." 1787. *Obras completas*. Ed. Felicidad Buendía. Vol. 1. Madrid: Aguilar, 1966. 784–91.
———. "Dedicatoria al Excelentísimo señor Conde-Duque." 1631. *Quevedo y su poética dedicada a Olivares: Estudio y edición*. Ed. Elías L. Rivers. Navarra: Universidad de Navarra, 1998. 37–57.
———. *España defendida y los tiempos de ahora*. 1609. *Obras completas*. Ed. Felicidad Buendía. Vol. 1. Madrid: Aguilar, 1966. 548–90.
———. *La Hora de todos y la Fortuna con seso*. 1650. Ed. Jean Bourg, Pierre Dupont, and Pierre Geneste. Madrid: Cátedra, 1987.
———. *Marco Bruto*. 1644. *Obras completas*. Ed. Felicidad Buendía. Vol. 1. Madrid: Aguilar, 1966. 915–91.
———. *Política de Dios: Govierno de Christo*. Part I. 1626. Part II. 1655. Ed. James Crosby. Urbana: University of Illinois Press, 1966.
———. *Prosa festiva completa*. Part I. 1626. Part II. 1655. Ed. Celsa Carmen García. Madrid: Cátedra, 1993.
———. *Los sueños: Sueños y discursos de verdades descubridoras de abusos, vicios y engaños en todos los oficios y estados del mundo*. 1627. Ed. Henry Ettinghausen. Barcelona: Planeta, 1990.
———. *La vida del Buscón llamado Don Pablos*. 1626. Ed. Domingo Ynduráin. Mexico City: REI, 1987.
Quijada, Mónica, and Jesús Bustamante, eds. *Élites intelectuales y modelos colectivos: Mundo ibérico (siglos XVI–XIX)*. Madrid: Consejo Superior de Investigaciones Científicas, 2002.
Redondo, Augustín. *Le corps dans la société espagnole des XVIe et XVIIe siècles: Colloque international*. Paris: Sorbonne, 1990.
Relacion de las fiestas que la ciudad de Huesca de el reyno de Aragon ha hecho al nacimiento del principe nuestro señor D. Felipe Prospero. Huesca: n.p., 1658.
Riandère La Roche, Josette. "Nota para una mejor comprensión de un texto de Quevedo: *La Hora de todos*." *Hommage des hispanistes français à Noel Salomon*. Barcelona: Laia, 1979. 725–32.
———. "La satire du 'Monde à L'envers' chez Quevedo." *L'image du monde renversé et ses représentations littéraires et para-littéraires de la fin du XVIe siècle au milieu du XVIIe*. Ed. Jean Lafond and Augustin Redondo. Paris: Vrin, 1979. 55–71.
Ricoeur, Paul. *Teoría de la interpretación: Discurso y excedente de sentido*. Trans. Graciela Monges Nicolau. Mexico City: Siglo XXI, 1995.
Rivadeneira, Pedro de. *Tratado de la religión y virtudes que debe tener el príncipe cristiano*. 1595. Madrid: Atlas, 1952.
Robbins, Jeremy. *Arts of Perception: The Epistemological Mentality of the Spanish Baroque, 1580–1720*. Abingdon: Routledge, 2007.
Roccabella, Tommaso. *El príncipe deliberante*. Trans. Sebastián de Ucedo. Milan: n.p., 1670.

Rodríguez de Monforte, Pedro. *Descripcion de las honras que se hicieron a la catholica Magestad de D. Phelippe quarto Rey de las Españas y del nueuo Mundo en el Real Conuento de la Encarnacion.* Madrid: Francisco Nieto, 1666.
Rodríguez Villa, Antonio. *Etiquetas de la casa de Austria.* Madrid: Ratés, 1913.
Saavedra Fajardo, Diego de. *Empresas políticas.* 1640. Madrid: Cátedra, 1999.
——. *Idea de un principe politico christiano representada en cien empresas.* Monaco: Nicolao Eurico, 1640.
——. *República literaria.* 1670. Bilbao: Plaza and Janés, 1985.
Santa María, Juan de. *Repvblica y policia christiana: Para reyes y principes y para los que en el gouierno tienen sus vezes.* Barcelona: Geronymo Margarit, 1617.
Schiller, Friedrich. *The Philosophical and Aesthetic Letters and Essays.* London: John Chapman, 1845.
Scholem, Gershom. *Major Trends in Jewish Mysticism.* New York: Schocken, 1941.
Schwartz Lerner, Lía. *Metáfora y sátira en la obra de Quevedo.* Madrid: Taurus, 1983.
Schwartz Lerner, Lía, and Antonio Carreira, eds. *Quevedo a nueva luz: Escritura y política.* Málaga: Universidad de Málaga, 1997.
Seneca, Lucius Annaeus [Seneca the Elder]. *Seneca ad Lucilium Epistulae Morales.* Trans. Richard M. Gummere. Vol. 3. London: William Heinemann, 1925.
——. *Suasoriae. Declamations.* Trans. M. Winterbottom. Vol. 2. Cambridge, Mass.: Harvard University Press, 1974. 484–611.
Shakespeare, William. *The Tragedy of King Lear.* Cambridge: Cambridge University Press, 1992.
Smith, Hilary Dansey. *Preaching in the Spanish Golden Age: A Study of Some Preachers of the Reign of Philip II.* Oxford: Oxford University Press, 1978.
Solórzano Pereira, Juan de. *Emblemata regio politica: In centuriam unam redacta, et commentariis illustrata.* 1653.
Soufas, Christopher. "The Sublime, the Beautiful, and the Imagination in Zorrilla's *Don Juan Tenorio*." *Modern Language Notes* 110.2 (1995): 302–19.
Spacks, Patricia Meyer. "Some Reflections on Satire." *Satire: Modern Essays in Cricticism.* Ed. Ronald Paulson. Englewood Cliffs, N.J.: Prentice-Hall, 1971. 360–78.
Spadaccini, Nicholas, and Luis Martín-Estudillo, eds. *Hispanic Baroques: Reading Cultures in Context.* Nashville: Vanderbilt University Press, 2005.
Spadaccini, Nicholas, and Jenaro Talens. "The Practice of Worldly Wisdom: Rereading Gracián from the New World Order." *Rhetoric and Politics: Baltasar Gracián and the New World Order.* Ed. Nicholas Spadaccini and Jenaro Talens. Minneapolis: University of Minnesota Press, 1997. ix–xxxii.
Stoichita, Victor. *Visionary Experience in the Golden Age of Spanish Art.* London: Reaktion, 1995.
Stradling, R. A. *Philip IV and the Government of Spain, 1621–1665.* Cambridge: Cambridge University Press, 1988.
Strier, Richard. "Against the Rules of Reason: Praise of Passion from Petrarch to Luther to Shakespeare to Herbert." *Reading the Early Modern Passions: Essays in the Cultural History of Emotion.* Ed. Gail Kern Paster, Katherine Rowe, and Mary Floyd-Wilson. Philadelphia: University of Pennsylvania Press, 2004. 23–42.
Tanner, Marie. *The Last Descendant of Aeneas: The Hapsburgs and the Mythic Image of the Emperor.* New Haven: Yale University Press, 1993.
Tesauro, Emanuele. *Il cannochiale aristotelico.* 1654. Turin: Editrice Artistica Piemontese, 2000.

Thomas à Kempis. *The Imitation of Christ*. 1418. Trans. Leo Sherley-Price. London: Penguin, 1952.
Thompson, I. A. A. *Crown and Cortes: Government, Institutions, and Representation in Early-Modern Castile*. Aldershot: Ashgate, 1993.
Tierno Galván, Enrique. *El tacitismo en las doctrinas políticas del siglo de oro español*. Murcia: Nogués, 1949.
Torre, Felipe de la. *Institutción de un rey christiano*. 1556. Exeter: Exeter, 1979.
Torrente Ballester, Gonzalo. *Sor María de Agreda: Selección*. Vol. 2. Madrid: Ediciones Fe, 1942.
Valtanás, Domingo de. *Confessionario mvy vtil y provechoso a todo Christiano, ansi para el confessor como para el penitente*. Anvers [Antwerp]: Casa de Guillermo Simón, 1556.
Vickers, Brian. *In Defence of Rhetoric*. Oxford: Clarendon, 1998.
Vilar Berrogain, Jean. *Literatura y economía: La figura del arbitrista en el siglo de oro*. Madrid: Revista de Occidente, 1973.
Villalpando, Juan Bautista de. *In Ezechielem explanationes, et apparatus urbis, ac templi Hierosolymitani, commentariis et imaginibus illustratus*. N.p.: n.p., 1596.
Viroli, Maurizio. *From Politics to Reason of State: The Acquisition and Transformation of the Language of Politics, 1250–1600*. Cambridge: Cambridge University Press, 1992.
Vivar, Francisco. *Quevedo y su España imaginada*. Madrid: Visor, 2002.
Vives, Juan Luis. "Fábula del hombre." *Diálogos*. 1518. Trans. Juan Francisco Alcina. Barcelona: Planeta, 1988. 155–62.
Warnke, Georgia. "Hermeneutics, Ethics, and Politics." *The Cambridge Companion to Gadamer*. Ed. Robert J. Dostal. Cambridge: Cambridge University Press, 2002. 87–101.
Weber, Max. *The Sociology of Religion*. Boston: Beacon, 1993.
Webster, Susan Verdi. *Art and Ritual in Golden-Age Spain: Sevillian Confraternities and the Processional Sculpture of Holy Week*. Princeton: Princeton University Press, 1998.
Wolin, Richard. *Walter Benjamin, an Aesthetic of Redemption*. Berkeley and Los Angeles: University of California Press, 1994.
Zevallos, Geronymo. *Arte real para el bven govierno de los reyes, y principes, y de sus vassallos*. 1623. Madrid: Centro de Estudios Políticos y Constitucionales, 2003.

INDEX

Page numbers in *italics* refer to illustrations.

absolutism, 40–41, 72
action, language and, 100–101
Agamben, Giorgio, 38, 99, 125
Agreda, Sor María, 70–71
agudeza, 90
Álamos de Barrientos, Baltasar, 9, 124
allegory, 44, 132–35
Anthony, Saint, 58
Apostolidès, Jean-Marie, 29, 52–53, 56, 72
arbitristas, 124–25
Aristotle, 34
artifice
    in *Fábula del homine*, 109
    of French and Spanish courts, 52–53
    Gracián on, 91
Artificial Man, 112–13
art(s). *See also* letters
    art-life fusion, 26–27, 34–35, 45
    imitation in, 59–60
    tradition and, 131–32
Augustine
    on interpretation of Scripture, 8
    on knowledge and moral worth, 4
    on memorization and repetition, 87
    on rhetoric, 33–34, 38, 58, 85
aura, 11, 36
authority
    Hobbes on, 112–13
    and humility of king, 70–71
Ávila, Juan de, 60

Barthes, Roland, 138
Bautista de Villalpando, Juan, 66
beauty, Gracián on, 91–92
Benjamin, Walter, 11, 27, 130–32, 134
Berger, Harry, 7, 9, 142 n. 6
Blanco, Mercedes, 90

body. *See also* "order of the body"
    in early modernity, 5–8
    of kings, 45–46, 70–72
    touch and, 63–64
Borges, Jorge Louis, 1, 104, 106, 137–38
Borja, Juan de, 60
Borromeo, Carlo, 86
Botero, Giovanni, 21, 113
Bourdieu, Pierre, 2, 25, 69
Bourg, Jean, 103
Bouza, Fernando, 23–24, 29
Brown, Jonathan, 28, 29
Brown, Peter, 58, 61
Buen Retiro Palace, 51–52
Burke, Peter, 29, 49, 111

Caesar, Julius, 82
Calderón de la Barca, Pedro, 64–67, 76–77, 133
Caravaggio, Michelangelo Merisi da, *62*
Cascardi, Anthony, 111
Castiglione, Baldesar, 91
Castilian, 75
Castilla, Gabriel, 37
Catholic Church, 16, 21, 58–59
Caussin, Nicolas, 31
centralization, 110–11
Cervantes, Miguel de, 122, 132, 137–38
Charles V, King, 21, 119
Chartier, Roger, 23–24, 25, 78
Christ Gives the Symbols of Power to Philip II in the Presence of Pope Gregory XIII (Wierix), 54–56, *56*
Christ king, 3, 22–24, 31–32, 70–72
Chrysostom, St. John, 34
Cicero, Marcus Tullius, 4, 79, 96–98
Clamurro, William, 24–25, 105

clock, as symbol, 108, 114
Coleridge, Samuel Taylor, 43–44
commodification, 124–27
communication
   Berger on, 142 n. 6
   bias toward, 2
   Christian rhetoric, 33–38
   image and words and, 4–5
   La Hora de todos and, 106
   in *Marco Bruto*, 79–80
   political, 28–29
   Quevedo and, 3, 138–39
   virility in, 82–83
   written, 81–82, 83–84, 107–8, 127–32, 139
Considerazioni sulla pittura (Mancini), 59–60
court
   artifice of, 52–53
   as center of societal rationalization, 110–11
   as theater, 28–31
Cross/Crucifixion, 31–32, 58–59
culture
   fall of politics and, 100–101
   print and, 130

Dante, 137–38
de Armas, Frederick, 122
deification of monarchs, 6–7, 17–21, 41–42
de Man, Paul, 43
Derrida, Jacques, 130
Descartes, René, 141 n. 2
Description de las honras que se hicieron a la catholica Magestad de D. Phelippe quarto (Rodríguez de Monforte), 119, *120*
discretion, 90–91
Don Quijote (Cervantes), 80, 132
Doubting Thomas (Caravaggio), *62*
Dream of Philip II (El Greco), 54–56, *55*
Dupont, Pierre, 103
Durán, Manuel, 3

eagles, 119
economic reform, 124–27
El Greco, 54–56, *55*
Elias, Norbert, 40
Elliott, John H., 21, 28, 29, 142 n. 8
Emblemata regio politica (de Solórzano Pereira), 15, *16*
empiricism, 110–11
Empresas políticas (Saavedra Fajardo)
   "Ex Fvmo in Lvcem" emblem, 130, *131*
   "His Polis" emblem, 116, *117*

"Lvdibria Mortis" emblem, 15, *17*
   state machine and, 114–16
   "Vni Reddatur" emblem, *115*
Enlightenment, 127
Erasmus, Desiderius, 122
Espinel, Vicente, 95
Eucharist, 64–69
Eucharistic Chariot (Unknown), *68*
excellence, 85–96
"Ex Fvmo in Lvcem" emblem, 130, *131*

Fábula del homine (Vives), 109
faith, versus speech and written word, 86
Felicitas, Saint, 58
Fernández de Córdoba, Gonzalo, 79
Fernández Santamaría, José, 77–78
Fernando el Católico, 79–80
Feros, Antonio, 29, 71
flagellants, 58–59
Forcione, Alban, 17, 89
Forsett, Edward, 113
Foucault, Michel, 137–38
Francis Xavier, Saint, 36
Freedberg, David, 59, 60–61
Fuentes, Carlos, 122

Gadamer, Hans Georg, 10–11, 26–27, 44, 59–60, 72
Geertz, Clifford, 29, 71
Geneste, Pierre, 103
Goffman, Erving, 91
Gómez de Reguera, Francisco, 74
Gongorism, 127–28
González Dávila, Gil, 4
González de Cellorigo, Martín, 21
Gospels, 26
grace, 64–66
Gracián, Baltasar, 2, 34–36, 80, 89–92, 127
Granada, Fray Luis de, 33–34
Greer, Margaret, 8
Guevara, Antonio de, 29, 108

Harvey, Elizabeth, 63
healing, through royal touch, 42
Heiple, Daniel, 108–9
Herrera, Fernando de, 75
"His Polis" emblem, 116, *117*
Hobbes, Thomas, 112–13
La Hora de todos y la Fortuna con seso
   communication and, 3
   financial reform and, 123–27
   introduction to, 100–106

learning and literacy and, 106–12
loss of allegory in, 132–35
rise of print and, 127–32
state machine and, 112–23
Host, 64, 66–67
Huarte de San Juan, Juan, 35, 86–88, 91
humility, 70–71
Hutson, Lorna, 41

Iffland, James, 105
Ignatius of Loyola, 5, 60, 61
illusionism, 76–77
image
  controlling, 76–77
  of royal courts, 52–53
  of rulers, 24–26, 49–52, 56, 73–78
  words and, 4–8, 34–35
imitatio Christi, 31–32, 42, 58–64, 67–69, 70

Juan de la Cruz, San, 38
Jáuregui y Aguilar, Juan de, 86
Jesus Christ. *See also* imitatio Christi
  authority of, 36–37, 39
  Christ king and, 3, 22–24, 31–32, 70–72
  ritual experience and, 29–31
  touching resurrected, 62–63
Jesús de la Pasión (Montañés), 64, 65
John I, King, 69

Kahn, Victoria, 57
Kamen, Henry, 21, 106–7
Kantorowicz, Ernst, 41
Kertzer, David, 60
King Lear (Shakespeare), 57, 110
King Philip II Offering His Son, Prince Ferdinand, to God After the Victory of Lepanto (Titian), 15, *18*
King Philip IV of Spain (de Velázquez), 15–16, *20*
kings/kingship
  addressing, 16–17
  artifice and political legitimacy and, 52–57
  authority and presence of, 2, 36–38, 45–49
  as *corpus mysticum*, 31–32
  deified, 6–7, 17–21
  Eucharist and, 64–69
  example for, 34–35
  financial reform and, 123–24
  humility and authority of, 70–72
  image of, 15–16, 24–26, 49–52
  imitatio Christi and, 61
  laws and, 38–44

modern state and, 21–22
paper king, 80–85
rituals of, 28–30
royal comportment for, 22–23
speech and, 73–78
touch and, 62–64

Lanaja, Martín de, 88
language
  action and, 100–101
  civic function and social power of, 75–76
  knowledge and, 44
  in *La Hora de todos*, 127–32
  Quevedo and, 137–38
Lascombes, André, 7
law, 38–45
León, Fray Luis de, 93–95, 127
Lerma, Duke of, 22, 40
Lerner, Lía Schwartz, 3
letters, 75–76, 100–101, 106–12, 118, 139
letter writing, 81–82, 83–84, 127–32
Leviathan (Hobbes), 112
Lezra, Jacques, 122, 132
Lida, Raimundo, 3
life-art fusion, 26–27, 34–35, 45
Lipsius, Justin, 80, 82
Longinus, 85
Louis XIV, King, 49, 50–51
"Lvdibria Mortis" emblem, 16, *17*

magnificence, 85–96
Mancini, Giulio, 59–60
Manuzio, Paolo, 85
Maravall, Antonio, 4
Marco Bruto
  communication and, 3
  excellence in, 85–96
  paper king and, 80–85
  Seneca the Elder's suasoriae and, 96–99
  speech in, 73–78
  structure and history of, 78–80
Mariana, Juan de, 40
Marin, Louis, 25
Mariscal, George, 3
Márquez, Juan, 71
McLuhan, Marshall, 110, 127, 129
memory/memorization, 87
Mendo, Andrés, 15, *16*
mercantilism, 124–27
modernization, 4, 106–7
Monanni, Bernardo, 52
Moncada, Sancho de, 9, 21–22, 123–24

Montañés, Juan Martínez, 64, 65
Most, Glenn, 62–63
Mouchel, Christian, 85, 88
Mulryne, J. R., 29
Muñoz, Agustín, 59
mystification, 71–72

Nadal, Jerónimo, 5
Navarrete, Ignacio, 75
Nebrija, Antonio de, 75–76
Noort, Juan de, 119, *121*
El nuevo palacio del Retiro (Calderón), 64–67
La Numancia (Cervantes), 122
Núñez de Castro, Alonso, 53
Núñez de Cepeda, Francisco, 119

Old Testament, 31–32, 43–44
Olivares, Count-Duke of
  Buen Retiro Palace and, 51
  "Dedicatoria al Excelentísimo señor Conde-Duque," 93–94
  on flexibility, 8
  Philip IV and, 69
  regime of, 22, 40, 48–49, 141 n. 4
Ong, Walter, 76, 143 n. 3
On the Sublime (Longinus), 85
oratory. *See also* rhetoric; speech
  Borromeo on, 86
  death of orator, 96–98
  influence of, 60
  in *Marco Bruto*, 78, 84, 93
  memory and, 87–88
  in Quevedo's era, 74–75
  in Quevedo works, 12, 13
"order of the body," 3, 7, 9, 26, 99
Ortega y Gasset, José, 126

Pacheco, Francisco, 15, 74, 119
Pagden, Anthony, 113
palace
  grace and, 64–66
  as theater, 28–31
paper king, 80–85
Paravicino, Hortensio, 31
Passion
  Eucharist and, 64–69
  historical process and, 52–57
  image of kings and, 49–52
  imitatio Christi and, 58–64
  introduction to, 47–49
Peraita, Carmen, 24–25
Perelman, Chaïm, 93

Pérez de Barradas, Francisco, 79–80
Pérez de Ledesma, Gonzalo, 85–86, 88–89
Philip II, King, 21, 31, 54–56, 72
Philip III, King, 48
Philip IV, King
  identification between Christ and, 69–71
  King Philip IV of Spain (de Velázquez), 15–16, *20*
  Olivares and, 141 n. 4
  Philip IV Flanked by Religion and Faith (de Noort), 119, *121*
  Política de Dios and, 22, 48–50
  Portrait of Philip IV as a Young Man (de Velázquez), 15–16, *19*
  redemption under, 54
Philip IV Flanked by Religion and Faith (de Noort), 119, *121*
physical contact, 62–64
Plato, 73
"Plus ultra," 119
Pocock, J. G. A., 32
Política de Dios: Govierno de Christo Part I
  Christian rhetoric in, 32–38
  Christ king in, 31–32
  communication and, 3
  court as theater in, 28–31
  kingship and law in, 38–46
  kingship in, 18–28
Política de Dios: Govierno de Christo Part II
  Eucharist and kingship in, 64–69
  imitatio Christi in, 58–64, 70–72
  introduction to, 47–49
  kingly image in, 49–52
  magnificence and redemption in, 52–57
Portocarrero y Guzmán, Pedro, 4, 77, 124
Portrait of Philip IV as a Young Man (de Velázquez), 15–16, *19*
pragmatism, 8–9, 81, 96, 107, 127
The Praise of Folly (Erasmus), 122
Premáticas, 83
print culture, 80, 107–8, 127–32, 139
prudencia, 8
Pulgar, Hernando del, 74
Pye, Christopher, 113

Racine, Jean, 56
Ramus, Petrus, 76
redemption, of kingdom, 54–57, 69
Relox de príncipes (de Guevara), 108
reputation, 73–78
response theory, 36
rex sacerdos, 31–32

rhetoric. *See also* oratory; speech
  Christian, 33–38, 43–44
  exceptional, 85–96
  of kings, 41–42
  La Hora de todos and, 106
  in *Marco Bruto*, 79–80
  Ong on, 143 n. 3
  in Quevedo's era, 74–76
Riandère La Roche, Josette, 105
Ricoeur, Paul, 26
ritual, 28–30, 60
Rivadeneira, Pedro de, 39
Roccabella, Tommaso, 73
Rodríguez de Monforte, Pedro, 119, *120*
Roman rhetoric, 33
royal ceremony, 28–30
royal touch, healing through, 42

Saavedra Fajardo, Diego de. *See also Empresas políticas* (Saavedra Fajardo)
  on exhibition of power, 41
  on humanities and science, 111–12
  on images for prince, 35
  on king's legal authority, 45
  on king's words, 73, 77
  pragmatism and, 127
  on secretary and bureaucratic documents, 82
Santa María, Juan de, 34, 40–41, 45
Schiller, Friedrich, 89
Scholem, Gershom, 44
scientific revolution, 6–7, 107, 108–9, 111–12
Scriptures, 26, 31–32, 43–44
sea power, 116
secretary, 82
self-restraint, 90–91
Seneca the Elder, 73, 79, 82–83, 96–99
Shakespeare, William, 57, 110
Shewring, Margaret, 29
"Sic Regat Rex Solvm" emblem, 15, *16*
silence, 77, 98
Socrates, 86
Solórzano Pereira, Juan de, 15, *16*
Spain
  centralization and, 110–11
  deified kings in, 41–42
  images of kingship in, 15–16
  increased literacy in, 107–8
  involvement and image of monarchs in, 24–26
  modernization and tradition in, 21–22, 106–7
  royal protocol in, 16–17
  scientific revolution in, 6, 108–9
  vivid exemplification in, 4–5
  weakened kingship in, 47–49
Spanish language, 75–76, 127–32, 137–38
speech. *See also* oratory; rhetoric
  exceptional, 85–96
  reputation and, 73–78
  virility in, 82–83
spyglass, 114–15
Stradling, R. A., 49
Strier, Richard, 57
suasoriae, of Seneca the Elder, 96–99
Synesius, 22

Tanner, Marie, 142 n. 8
Tesauro, Emanuele, 35
theater, court as, 28–31
Thomas (apostle), 62–63
Thomas à Kempis, 60
Titian, 15, *18*
touch, 62–64
tradition, 106–7, 131–32
Trauerspiel, 11, 134
Turpilius, 82
"typographic man," 127–32

Valencia, Andrés de, 6
Valtanás, Domingo de, 58, 60
vander Hammen, Lorenço, 36, 37–38
Vázquez de Menchaca, Fernando, 113
Velázquez, Diego de, 15–16, *19, 20*
vellón, 124, 125
Vickers, Brian, 36
vir bonus dicendi peritus, 85–96
virtù/virtue, 78, 82, 84
Vives, Juan Luis, 76, 109
"Vni Reddatur" emblem, 114, *115*

Watanabe-O'Kelly, Helen, 29
Weber, Max, 32
Webster, Susan Verdi, 59
Wierix, Jeronimus, 54–56, *56*
Willughby, Francis, 107
Wolin, Richard, 134
words. *See also* rhetoric
  image and, 4–8, 34–35
  imitatio Christi and, 60
  of king, 73–78
  virility in, 82–83
written communication, 80–84, 107–8, 127–32, 139

www.ingramcontent.com/pod-product-compliance
Lightning Source LLC
Chambersburg PA
CBHW031553300426
44111CB00006BA/292